Control Units and Supermaxes: A National Security Threat

Joseph Dole

Control Units and Supermaxes: A National Security Threat

By Joseph Rodney Dole, II

Self-Published with assistance from
MIDNIGHT EXPRESS BOOKS

Joseph Rodney Dole II

Control Units and Supermaxes: A National Security Threat

ISBN-13 978-1533213808

ISBN-10: 1533213801

Self-Published with assistance from
MIDNIGHT EXPRESS BOOKS
POBox 69
Berryville AR 72616
(870) 210-3772
MEBooks1@yahoo.com

Control Units and Supermaxes: A National Security Threat

By Joseph Rodney Dole, II

-DEDICATION-

This book is dedicated to all those (like Tamms Year Ten) who fight to end long-term solitary confinement, and to all those suffering in isolation chambers around the country and world. It is especially dedicated to all those who continue to resist oppression, fight for their rights, and demand to be treated humanely.

Joseph Rodney Dolell

-INTRODUCTION-

Beginning in the 1960s, control units, then later supermax prisons, popped up from coast to coast as if part of a fast food franchise.

There was almost no outcry over this. Little known outside of correctional circles, barely a peep was uttered in opposition. Analyzing the costs versus the benefits of building them was unheard of. Nor did anyone consider any moral, ethical, or humanitarian downsides of building them.

Recently however, more and more conscientious people are starting to realize that there are, in fact, great risks associated with building these facilities and isolating thousands of people (men, women, and children), some for decades. People are now recognizing that, rather than being the legitimate security tool they were billed as, they actually pose a significant threat to society.

Contents

Joseph Rodney Dolell

-HISTORY-

In 2007, the International Psychological Trauma Symposium was held in Istanbul, Turkey. It adopted "The Istanbul Statement on the Use and Effects of Solitary Confinement", which lists four criminal justice circumstances around the world in which solitary confinement is used:

> As…a disciplinary punishment for sentenced prisoners; for the isolation of individuals during an ongoing criminal investigation; increasingly as an administrative tool for managing specific groups of prisoners; and as judicial sentencing. In many jurisdictions solitary confinement is also used as a substitute for proper medical or psychiatric care for mentally disordered individuals (Istanbul Statement, 2007:p.63).

Solitary confinement has existed in some form or another for centuries. Citing the *American Encyclopedia*, the United States Supreme Court noted in an 1890 opinion that "the first plan adopted [using solitary confinement as punishment for crime]...was the solitary prison connected with the Hospital San Michele at Rome, in 1703"(In re Medley, 1890:p. 167-168, 386). Similar to the isolation units today, the Court noted that it too was "little known" (Ibid.). America began its first experiments with solitary confinement shortly after the birth of the country. In 1787, solitary confinement was used in the Walnut Street Penitentiary in Philadelphia (Ibid.). Just three years later, "[i]n 1790, legislation authorized the construction of 16 small individualized cells at Walnut Street...where prisoners were kept in isolation" (Friedmann, 2012:p.1).

According to Sharon Shalev, who compiled *A Sourcebook On Solitary Confinement*, it was the "Boston Prison Disciplinary Society which helped devise the 'Separate' or 'Pennsylvania' system of solitary confinement" (Shalev, 2008:p.10). Under this system, "prisoners were held in solitary confinement and segregated from each other almost all of the time, including during meals. The Pennsylvania System was intended to induce penitence and reformation by providing prisoners with time alone to contemplate their sins" (Friedmann, 2012:p.l). Philadelphia was also home to America's "first prison exclusively dedicated to solitary confinement" (Tietz, 2012:p.3). This was the Eastern State Penitentiary which was built in 1829 and served "as a model for more than 300 prisons in the United States and Europe" (Ibid.).

After decades of experience with solitary confinement though, people realized that "instead of its intended role of helping to 'cure the disease of crime', solitary confinement was creating illness in prisoners" (Friedmann, 2012:p.l0). This "played a central role in the dismantling of the isolation prisons on both sides of the Atlantic by the late 19th Century" (Ibid.). Although solitary confinement was still used as a management tool of the prison system, entire prisons dedicated to iso-lation didn't reappear until the latter half of the 20th Century.

The impetus for the return of prisons using large-scale isolation - the efficacy of which had been disproven decades earlier - was manifold.

The return began with the control unit. Basically, the control unit is a prison inside a prison where all inmates are in solitary confinement of one kind or another (Kamel and Kerness, 2003). As Bonnie Kerness noted in *WIN Magazine*, "one of the first control units was established in the late 1960s" (Kerness, 2009:p.21). It was located in San Quentin Prison's 0 Wing (Ibid.). It is commonly misreported that the first such unit was at the Marion Federal Penitentiary in Illinois in 1972 (Magnani, 2008). This can be attributed to how well these units are kept hidden from the public. Marion established their "infamous H-Unit, made up of cruel boxcar cells" (Kerness, 2009:p.21), after a guard was killed that year (Magnani, 2008). Numerous other states such as New Jersey and Massachusetts also established similar control units in existing prisons around the same time (Kerness, 2009:p.21).

The rationale for these units was that a small portion of the prison population was uncontrollably violent and had to be kept isolated and secured to protect both staff and other inmates. Once established though, prison administrators expanded the criteria to include: anyone they label as a gang member; jailhouse lawyers who garner the animosity of the administration by filing grievances or lawsuits in order to protect their civil rights; anyone they think might commit a staff assault; inmates who require protection from other inmates; illegal immigrants; and inmates who continuously break prison rules. More often than not, the latter are mentally ill people who are incapable of following such a strict regimen. Most people still think of only men being subjected to isolation, but America spares neither women nor children this punishment. Although placing children in solitary confinement is a violation of international law (Clark and Maki, 2014), the practice is all too common in the United States (Liebelson, 2015). From California to Florida, hundreds of women also languish in solitary confinement (Law, 2014: p.12). Often it is because they are victims of sexual assault by guards (Ibid.: p. 14). When they report the assault, they are labeled trouble-makers as part of the cover-up and isolated in retaliation. Therefore, solitary confinement can go by many names - - Disciplinary Segregation, Administrative Detention, Protective Custody, etc. This is done in an attempt to disguise them from the public, but also makes it difficult to collect data.

Beginning in the 1970s, tough-on-crime rhetoric blossomed throughout the country. Accompanying this rhetoric were laws that made more crimes punishable with imprisonment and extended sentences and/or the percentage of time people must serve in prison. This resulted in severe overcrowding in prisons throughout the country. Additionally, the country's hatred of prisoners caused it to abandon most attempts at rehabilitation. Therefore, most educational, vocational, and re-entry programs disappeared, leaving prisoners idle.

Furthermore, as Art Leonardo, the executive director of the North American Association of Wardens and Superintendents, noted, "We began in this country to stop institutionalizing people who had mental illnesses. We just put them in jail. Jails are really not prepared or staffed in most cases to deal with them" (Associated Press, 2012). Add to this toxic brew the passage of the Prison Litigation Reform Act. This decimated a prisoners' ability to seek redress for violation of their constitutional rights, thereby encouraging prison administrators and guards to violate those rights. All of these factors contributed to rising levels of violence inside prisons.

Writing on the *Bangor Daily News* website, Terry Kupers and David Moltz explain that:

> There was good research showing that overcrowding and idleness result in sharp rises in the rates of violence, psychiatric breakdown and suicide in prisons. But instead of alleviating overcrowding, re-instituting rehabilitation, and finding somewhere that individuals suffering from mental illness could receive needed treatment, authorities took a wrong turn and reacted to the rising violence by locking down prisoners they castigated as "the worst of the worst" in their solitary cells (Kupers and Moltz, 2010).

Over the next three decades, the nation went on a prison-building spree to try to keep up with the unprecedented increase in the prison population. Along with the increase in prisoners and prisons came an increase in the number of prisoners who the administration deemed required isolation. Therefore, not only did control units expand and multiply, but an entirely new segment of the prison-building industry was created - the design and building of entire prisons dedicated to the complete isolation and control of prisoners. These prisons took on the name "supermax".

The first supermax was Marion. Instead of being built from scratch though, it was an existing prison converted to pure solitary confinement in 1983 "when the whole facility went on lockdown after two guards were murdered there" (Felshman, 2008). Shortly thereafter, the Bureau of Prisons (BOP) built the first contemporary prison dedicated solely to being a completely controlled environment when it built the ADX in Florence, Colorado (Eisenman and Reynolds, 2009). By 1997 - the year that "California opened a supermax at Pelican Bay State Prison" (Felshman, 2008), and construction was completed on Tamms Supermax Prison less than an hour's drive from Marion in Illinois - all but five states in the union, along with the District of Columbia, were operating control units, supermax prisons, or both (Kamel and Kerness, 2003: p.2; Kerness, 2009: p.21; and Magnani, 2008: p.3) .

The nation is now to the point that, although solitary confinement has been around for centuries, we use it more often and for longer periods of time than anyone else in the world ever has. Never before has it been used on such a massive scale and with such indifference towards the consequences for society at large. Although there were hundreds of prisons in the 19th Century that used solitary confinement as their model, none of them were on a scale that they are today. Mass incarceration is a current phenomenon, and so too is mass use of isolation, where tens of thousands of people are isolated for years or even decades.

-NUMBERS -

Just as it is difficult to identify all of the different segregation units, control units, and supermaxes around the country (which governments and correctional agencies work so hard to keep out of view of the public), so too is it difficult to obtain concrete numbers on how many people are in these isolation chambers on any given day or in any given year.

On the low end of the spectrum, Human Rights Watch calculated that nearly 2% of the prison population, or 20,000 people are in isolation in the U. S. (Magnani, 2008: p.4; Kamel and Kerness, 2003: p.2; and Kerness, 2009: p.21). Similarly, in 2009 the American Friends Service Committee estimated it was as high as 2.5% (Kerness, 2009: p.21), and the Urban Institute put the number at 25,000 in 2006 (Friedmann, 2012: p.3). *Harper's* Magazine, citing the ACLU, says 1 in 27 prisoners are in solitary (*Harper's*, 2012a:p.l3). The *Bangor Daily News* reports 3% to 10% (Kupers and Moltz, 2010), and *Solitary Watch* claims 4% to 8% "are consigned to segregation or isolation" (Ridgeway and Casella, 2012).

On the high end of the spectrum, the Coalition For Prisoners' Rights (CFPR), reported in 2010 that on "any given day, as many as 100,000 people are living in solitary confinement in U.S. prisons" (Coalition For Prisoners' Rights, 2010a: p.l).

The most commonly cited figure though, is around 80,000 (CFPR, 2010b; Tapley, 2012: p.16; Friedman, 2012: p.3), which seems to originate with the Bureau of Justice Statistics which found that 80,870 were in segregation in 2000 - 36,499 in administrative segregation, 10,735 in protective custody, and 33,586 in disciplinary segregation (Gibbons and de B. Katzenbach, 2006:p.56). The problem with this is that many states, like Illinois, fail to respond to the BOJ's surveys and never, or infrequently, report their own statistics due to a complete lack of competent staff or resources to compile them in the first place. Another problem with keeping track of the number of people in isolation is the rapid growth of this population and the lag time in reporting. For instance, in 2010, the CFPR, citing a study by The Commission on Safety and Abuse in America's Prisons, reported that "the number of prisoners in solitary confinement grew 40% from 1995 to 2000 - when there were 80,870 such segregated prisoners," while the prison population as a whole grew by 28% (CFPR, 2010b:p.l). So a decade later, sources still cite to 2000 statistics while the prison population is growing.

The 20,000 - 25,000 numbers are definitely too low. California alone had over 14,000 in solitary confinement by 2008 (Magnani, 2008:p.6). "[Seven] percent of federal prisoners are housed in segregation units - which, based on the BOP's current [2012] estimates equates to around 15,000 prisoners" (Friedmann, 2012:p.3). Texas still has over 8,000 in administrative segregation units (Ibid:p.8). Suffice it to say, many tens, if not hundreds, of thousands of Americans are being held in isolation on any given day around the country.

-CONDITIONS-

By far the worst prison environments in the U.S. are found in control units and supermax prisons. Think Guantanamo Bay, but often worse. Amazingly, the level of outrage expressed over mistreating Americans in U.S. prisons has been miniscule compared to society's uproar over how foreign nationals were treated in Guantanamo Bay or Abu Ghraib. A public that would normally punish any politician who suggests closing any prison, had no qualms about electing a president who promised to close down Guantanamo Bay. The disconnect is curious. Do we really hate our own citizens who commit a crime more than we hate people who want to wipe America off the map? It seems we do.

As *Solitary Watch* reported, "[m]illions of Americans have been haunted by the specter of Guantanamo Bay and Abu Ghraib where isolation and deprivation have been raised to the level of torture. Yet every day, here in the United States, tens of thousands of prisoners languish" in similar environments (Ridgeway and Casella, 2011:p.l). President Obama claims "we don't torture," yet according to *The Capital City Courier* the "prototype for the sealed off and fortress-like Camps 5 and 6 at Guantanamo Bay" was "the prison at Florence [ADX] - along with dozens of similar super-high security facilities in the U.S." (Eiseman and Reynolds, 2009). The authors noted that there are dozens and perhaps as many as a hundred Guantanamo Bays right here in the United States. Just as we tortured people in Guantanamo Bay, so too do we torture people in the stateside Guantanamos.

The United Nations also disagrees with President Obama's claim that "we don't torture." The American Friends Service Committee - Arizona (AFSC - Arizona) notes how:

> United nations committees have specifically cited U.S.
> supermax prison units for violations of international

human rights laws. In 1995, a U.N. report criticized the United States for operating 'inhumane and degrading' prisons, and specifically cited detention facilities such as California's Pelican Bay State Prison....[I]n May of 2000, the U.N. Committee Against Torture called the 'excessively harsh regime' of supermax prisons a violation of the Convention Against Torture and made it clear that the practice is widespread in the U.S. (Isaacs and Lowen, 2007).

This is because "[u]nder international standards for human rights, extended isolation is banned as a form of torture" (Kamel and Kerness, 2003: p.4). Even guards at Guantanamo Bay agree that prisons in the U.S. are worse. Writing in the magazine *Smithsonian*, Joseph Lelyveld recounted how when he visited Guantanamo in 2002:

> Many of the guards had worked as correctional officers in their civilian lives. When I asked to meet some of them I was introduced to two women normally employed in state prisons in Georgia. The harsh conditions in which the supposed terrorists were held, they told me, were a little harder than normal "segregation" for troublesome prisoners in the Georgia system, but not nearly so hard as Georgia-style "isolation". I took this to be expert testimony (Lelyveld, 2011:p. 62).

So, just what are the physical conditions like in these control units and supermax prisons? Although they vary from one to the next, nearly all have the following in common: the prisoner is obviously isolated in a one-man cell, and both meals and exercise are solitary affairs (Kamel and Kerness, 2003:p. 2); all communication with the outside world - through mail, telephone calls, and visits with family (and maybe friends) - is severely curtailed (Ibid.); reading material is highly censored and privileges such as access to art supplies and education programs are usually rare if not non-existent.

There is usually little or no public oversight of these units or prisons because they are "carefully hidden from public view, intentionally located in isolated... rural areas" (Dowker and Good, 1993:p. 107). At times, the courts have described the conditions as "ghastly," "sordid and horrible," "depressing in the extreme," and, more recently, constituting an "atypical and significant hardship" compared to ordinary prison life (Westefer, 2010).

The AFSC-Oakland notes how prisoners are confined alone in:

> Cells [that] contain only the most basic of accommodations... a bed, a toilet and sink, and possibly another protruding slab for a desk.... Most cells have no windows.... Prisoners eat alone in their cells... "shake-downs" are common, and prisoners are routinely strip searched before leaving their cells (Magnani, 2008:p. 4).

Many of these prisons or units are creating "their own innovations controlling and dehumanizing prisoners," such as the control unit in Corcoran where "armed guards patrol the Plexiglas ceilings over the cells and peer in at the prisoners through Plexiglas cell walls" (Dowker and Good, 1993:p. 97; citing Wilson, 1991:p. 2).

Human contact is either totally non-existent, or nearly so, and can last for decades. Even when escorted by guards, prisoners are held tightly by hands covered in either leather gloves or rubber surgical gloves. There is usually no exception to the rule prohibiting contact visits. Attorney Jean Snyder told an Illinois House Committee how:

> One little girl who was dying of cancer told the Make A Wish Foundation that she wanted to visit her father at Tamms [Supermax Prison] and hug him one last time. The Foundation wished that she would pick a trip to Disney World - but she didn't. So the Foundation paid for the girl's visit to Tamms, where the girl saw her father through a glass booth and could not hug or kiss him (Snyder, 2001).

One of the limited privileges that most prisoners in isolation retain is the opportunity to go to "yard." The reason being is that prisoners have a right to exercise, which is protected by the 8th Amendment to the U.S. Constitution. Unfortunately, "yard" is usually a misnomer. The "yards" found in control units and supermaxes are almost universally less square footage than a semitrailer, and are made out of either thick gauge wire mesh walls and ceiling, or are simply a large cement tomb with twenty-feet-high walls and a chain link fence for a roof to allow light in. There are usually no weights or sports equipment, so the only exercise one gets is calisthenics.

These yards are commonly referred to as "dog runs". These dog runs always have cameras for constant surveillance, but almost never have access to water or a toilet. "Yard time" is routinely cancelled for the most arbitrary of reasons - too hot, too cold, ice on the ground, snow on the ground, too foggy, camera not functioning, it's thundering, lightning, raining too hard, etc.

During summers in Tamms, the cement walls and floors of the yards were graffitied with bird feces. Those weren't the only feces that found their way onto the yards either. Mentally ill inmates would often smear feces on the walls. Additionally, inmates, especially elderly ones, feared being stranded on the yard and losing control of their bladder or bowels. When it occurred, other inmates felt a flood of conflicting emotions when they learned that someone defecated on the yard. They were angry at staff for ignoring the inmate's pleas to be let in to use the bathroom; and also angry over the fact that they now couldn't go to yard unless they were willing to share a confined space with another man's feces - the thought of which alone engendered disgust. On the other end of the emotional spectrum though, inmates would feel sympathy for the often elderly gentleman who was both incontinent and embarrassed, and who was reduced to begging guards a third or a half of his age to be permitted to use the washroom, only to be ignored and then ridiculed as the guy who shit himself. Then there was also the possibility that he would be written a disciplinary ticket or even stripped of normal meals and served only what is known as "mealloaf." Each disciplinary infraction would furthermore be used to justify continued placement in Tamms.

Peaceful protests are likewise not tolerated. For instance, inmates who went on a hunger strike in protest of the inhumane conditions in Tamms, would often find themselves in the most nonsensical chain of events. When an inmate declared a hunger strike, staff would immediately shake down his cell and remove all commissary or other food items to ensure he was actually starving himself. This included toothpaste. Prison officials claimed that prisoners can survive by eating toothpaste. Such a claim is hard to swallow though when one considers that nearly all toothpaste packages bear a warning that reads something like: "If more than used for brushing is accidentally swallowed, seek professional help or contact a Poison Control Center immediately." Supermax inmates were seemingly superhuman - they could survive by consuming poison. With strict property limits, the amount of toothpaste an inmate possessed constituted less than two ounces.

Now, one might think the toothpaste may have been confiscated so that they couldn't poison themselves, but that wasn't the case. No other "poisonous" substances were ever confiscated, and nor were the prisoners placed on suicide watch. The guards just thought it amusing that they could add to the suffering. "What's worse than starving? Starving with 'yuck mouth'," the guards would taunt, laughing as they waved the toothpaste upon exiting the cell.

If the prisoner lasted 10 days without eating though, he would then be forcibly removed from his cell, and taken to the Health Care Unit. There, a rubber hose would be forced up his nose and down his throat so that staff could force-feed him. This was all written policy and procedure at Tamms - first ensure he can't eat, then forcibly and violently feed him.

In Illinois, it used to be that prison officials needed a court order to force-feed someone. On January 2, 2005 that changed. Illinois enacted a law which became effective immediately, called the "Hunger Strike Statute". Tamms' inmates were informed of it 10 days later in Warden's Bulletin No. 05-06. It read: "a law has been enacted regarding hunger strikes which allows us to force feed inmates without a court order" (Frey, 2005).

Furthermore, the unwritten policy at Tamms when an inmate went on hunger strike, was to cut off his communications with the outside world to prevent him from publicizing his strike, and prevent bringing attention to the heinous conditions and/or his unjust treatment. Often he would discover that his mail had been "lost" or delayed until after his strike ended.

All of this was designed to deprive him of the only peaceful means a prisoner has to protest his inhumane treatment. Similar tactics are utilized in control units and supermaxes around the country.

Take California for example, for the first three weeks of July, 2011 over 7,000 inmates protested, including those held in the state's Secure Housing Units (SHUs) (California's name for its control units and supermaxes). According to *Prison Health News*, "[h]unger strikers said that medications they had previously received were being denied as punishment" (Subways, 2011), and the *Los Angeles Times* was being denied access to interview participants.

Speaking of hunger, let's return to the subject of "mealloaf". A common punishment employed in supermaxes and control units is to feed inmates "mealloaf" - an entire meal ground up and baked into a hard loaf. Prisoners can barely stomach it so they often go hungry instead. At Tamms, the list of justifications for placing an inmate on mealloaf was exhaustive, as Warden's Bulletin No. 99-88 made clear:

> Inmates who display inappropriate behavior such as throwing food items or utensils, containers, trays, failure to return or properly dispose of uneaten food, drink items, serving utensils, containers or trays, obstruction or preventions of the closure of the food passage [(chuckhole)], spitting, throwing, making weapons, or improper disposal of human waste discharge or fluids MAY be placed on controlled feeding status (Mealloaf)(Welborn, 1999).

Any form of protest, like refusing to return a meal tray, is used against the protester. As Dr. Rhodes notes, "[b]ehavior in prison...has increasingly come to be understood primarily as a matter of individual choice divorced from its social context. Thus, for example, a super-maximum prisoner deprived of all but the most minimal options is offered the 'choice' of returning a meal tray or keeping it in his cell as a gesture of defiance. Defiant behavior is then cited as proof that this form of confinement is necessary" (Rhodes, 2005:p. 1692) .

In addition to being forced to endure all of the previously-mentioned conditions, there is also no intellectual stimulation. The AFSC's Bonnie Kerness writes that access to educational or therapeutic programs like G.E.D. or college courses, AA groups, or counseling is non-existent (Magnani, 2008:p. 4; Kerness, 2009:p. 21). About the only education a prisoner in isolation can obtain is through self-education. However, even self-education is largely out of reach for the large percentage of inmates who are illiterate, have learning disabilities like Attention Deficit Disorder or Dyslexia, or lack the resources to obtain the necessary materials.

There are also different levels of conditions inside supermaxes. So, although the conditions described above are found in most of them, in certain units or wings of supermaxes, it can be much worse. For instance, inmates may be denied clothes, a mattress, or property for days or weeks at a time; experience daily cell extractions; etc. Supermax prisons and control units have been called the "prisons within the prisons" (Kamel and Kerness, 2003). Elevated security wings though, are like the prisons within the prisons within the prisons. This is where many of the severely mentally ill wind up. Cell walls are often smeared with blood and feces, and many cells are reserved specifically for inmates on suicide watch.

Then there are the torture devices. These may include five-point restraints, restraint hoods, restraint belts, restraint beds, stun grenades, stun guns, stun belts, tethers, chemical agents, waist chains, and more. Although torture devices may be used against any inmate in a control unit or supermax prison depending on their behavior, those on the elevated security wings seem to receive the majority of this type of abuse. As noted in *WIN Magazine*, "[i]solation units, supermax prisons, sensory deprivation, brutality toward prisoners, and the use of devices of torture are all violations of human rights and of fundamental human decency" (Kerness, 2009:p. 23). These practices are even more nefarious when used against the mentally ill and the perpetrators conspire to keep it from becoming public knowledge.

Caroline Isaacs and Matthew Lowen expressed "concern about abuse in these units involving physical restraints, chemical agents, stun guns and other forms of cruelty" (2007:p. 14); adding that:

> [f]rom the time AFSC began monitoring control units, reports from prisoners have indicated that they are operated with an extreme level of brutality. According to Kamel and Kerness, reports from Arizona state prisons stood out early on, with one describing a prisoner being shocked with a taser twenty-two times before dying. Others describe prisoners being exposed to pepper spray and then made to lie down on the gro-und outdoors in the Arizona sun, so that the heat and

sweat reactivated the chemical agent.... Pepper spray has become ubiquitous in correctional settings. The substance "inflames the mucous membranes, causing closing of eyes, coughing, gagging, shortness of breath, and an acute burning sensation on the skin and inside the nose and mouth" (Ibid:p. 14-15; citing Cusac, 2000).

During cell extraction "prisoners are confronted with four to six riot-clad officers, batons drawn, descending upon the prisoner, often hog-tying him/her, and removing him/her from the cell" (Magnani, 2008:p.4). This is almost always prefaced by macing or pepper spraying the inmate.

Living in such conditions for years or even decades is, to say the least, not pleasant, and severely affects those subjected to them. It not only constitutes a serious threat to the inmates, but as we'll see below, also to staff working in those units and supermaxes, and to society as well.

-THREAT TO INMATES-

Prolonged isolation poses significant risks to the wellbeing of inmates. It threatens both a person's mental and physical health, and can even increase the amount of time one spends incarcerated during their life. As Andrew Cohen wrote in the *Atlantic Monthly*, "It is indisputable, the scientists now say, that putting people into prolonged isolation jeopardizes their ability to ever assimilate back into society once they are released" (Cohen, 2014; citing Stromberg, 2014). All of these threats stem from the mental deterioration associated with enduring solitary confinement.

Supermax supporters like to brush off claims that solitary confinement can cause harm as nothing more than the delusional fabrications of prisoners and bleeding-heart liberals. The reality is that in both the scientific and medical communities, there is no doubt that solitary confinement is harmful. "There are three acknowledged experts [in this field]: Drs. Stuart Grassian, Craig Haney, and Terry Kupers" (Ridgeway and Casella, 2012).

Isaacs and Lowen relay how:

> According to psychologist Craig Haney the assertion that solitary confinement results in "harmful consequences" and "negative psychological effects" is based upon studies spanning four decades and multiple continents (Ill-Equiped, 2003). Put succinctly isolation is not healthy for any human being, regardless of the reason behind his or her isolation (Isaacs and Lowen, 2007:p. 19).

They go on to reiterate that "there is a wealth of well-recognized research that clearly demonstrates how solitary confinement for any extended amount of time can cause and exacerbate mental illness" (Ibid.). Writing on the subject of Maine prisoners in solitary confinement for *The Bangor Daily News*, Dr. Kupers, along with David Moltz, explain how:

> It is stunning how pervasive a known set of symptoms in this population are, including massive free-floating anxiety, incessant cleaning or pacing the cell, paranoid ideas, sleep disturbances, problems concentrating and remembering....The isolation and idleness that cause psychiatric symptoms in relatively healthy prisoners cause psychotic breakdowns, severe affective disorders and suicidal crisis in prisoners with histories of serious mental illness (Kupers and Moltz, 2010).

Dr. Grassian testified before the Commission on Safety and Abuse in United States Prisons, that "[i]t has in fact long been known that severe restriction of environmental and social stimulation has a profoundly deleterious effect on mental functioning" (Isaacs and Lowen, 2007:p. 19).

As far back as the 1800s it was recognized that prolonged isolation can have serious negative consequences for the people subjected to it. The U.S. Supreme Court noted in 1890 (about a somewhat more severe form of isolation than what is practiced today) that:

> A considerable number of prisoners fell, after even a short confinement, into a semi-fatuous condition, from which it was next to impossible to arouse them, and others became violently insane; others still, committed suicide; while those who stood the ordeal better were not generally reformed, and in most cases did not recover sufficient mental activity to be of any subsequent service to the community" (In re Medley, 1890).

Although the isolation practiced today may not be quite as harsh as it was in the 19th Century, the resulting harm to inmates is nearly the same. Sharon Shalev attempted to catalog the myriad symptoms or effects of prolonged isolation in her *Sourcebook on Solitary*

Confinement: emotional damage, nervousness, anxiety, appetite and/or weight loss, headaches, dizziness, confusion, difficulty with thinking, trouble concentrating, decline in mental functioning, trouble remembering, visual and auditory hallucinations, visual disturbances, heart palpitations, hypersensitivity to noises, claustrophobia, apathy, withdrawal, depersonalization, ruminations, detachment from reality and other psychoses, delusions, paranoia, feeling of constant persecution, severe depression, problems with impulse control, problems sleeping, nightmares, irrational anger, rage, and more (Shalev, 2008).

In Europe in the 1970s, they termed the collection of symptoms one acquired through long-term isolation as "separation syndrome" (lbid.:p. 11). These "included emotional, cognitive, social and physical problems" (Ibid.). The Vera Institute of Justices's report *Confronting Confinement* tells how: "[i]n the mid-1980s, psychiatrist Stuart Grassian studied a small group of Massachusetts prisoners who had been living in isolation. He identified a constellation of symptoms that includes overwhelming anxiety, confusion and hallucination, and sudden, violent and self-destructive outbursts. Because those prisoners were confined in the Secure Housing Unit, he called the effects 'SHU Syndrome," (Gibbons and de B. Katzenbach, 2006:p. 58; citing Grassian, 1983). According to psychologist Craig Haney and Mona Lynch, from the 1970s through 1997, there wasn't "a single study of nonvoluntary solitary confinement for more than 10 days that did not document negative psychiatric symptoms in its subjects" (Gibbons and de B. Katzenbach, 2006:p. 58; citing Haney and Lynch, 1997).

One factor that increases the risks of adverse mental health effects is something employed by nearly every supermax and control unit in the country—simply refusing to inform the prisoner of the duration of their isolation (Szilak, 2012:p. 7). This is especially hard for inmates in their twenties or thirties serving life sentences. It poses the real possibility that they will have to endure such conditions for four or five decades before dying alone of old age. Additionally, if periodic reviews are conducted concerning their placement in isolation (a practice usually entailing nothing more than an arbitrary, rubber-stamping "denial" process) they will relive the disappointment of a denial of release hundreds of times. As we'll see ahead, the other option - suicide - is often more appealing, and not just for lifers.

Many of the symptoms of long-term isolation are also symptoms of schizophrenia, and some supermax inmates end up being diagnosed as such by psychologists (Pawlacyzyk and Hundsdorfer, 2009a). Although it is unclear whether isolation can cause schizophrenia, it does seem plausible. Schizophrenia is "[a] psychosis marked by withdrawal from reality and by variable emotional, behavioral, or intellectual disturbances" (*American Heritage Dictionary*, 2001:p. 743), all of which are also symptoms of isolation. Shalev reported that:

> One study found support for the hypothesis that the "shut in" or "seclusive" personality, "generally considered to be the basis of schizophrenia may be the result of an extended period of 'cultural isolation,' that is, separation from intimate and sympathetic social contact" (Faris, 1962: 155). Faris added that "seclusiveness is frequently the last stage of a process that began with exclusion or isolation which was not the choice of the patient" (Ibid. at p. 159).

> Deprived of meaningful and sympathetic social contact and interaction with others the prisoner in solitary confinement may withdraw and regress. Even when isolated prisoners do not show any obvious symptoms, upon release from isolation they can become uncomfortable in social situations and avoid them, with negative consequences for subsequent social functioning in both the prison community and the outside community, again undermining the likelihood of successful resettlement (Shalev, 2008:p. 18-19;

citing Faris, 1962).

The evidence supporting the fact that isolation severely affects one's mental health is not solely testimonial and empirical. There is also solid evidence in the form of recordings of electroencephalogram (EEG) activity in the brain. According to *Solitary Watch*," one study found that a single week in solitary produced a change in EEG activity related to stress and anxiety. There's evidence that long-term isolation profoundly alters the brain chemistry..." (*Solitary Watch Newsletter*, 2011:p.3). Jeff Tietz likewise reported in *Rolling Stone* that "[a]fter a few days in solitary, the EEG readings of prisoners predictably shift, in the words of one researcher, toward 'an abnormal pattern characteristic of stupor and delirium - the 'semi-fatuous' state condemned by the U.S. Supreme Court in 1890" (Tietz, 2012:p.64). Citing a study by Scott and Gendreau published in 1969 in the *Canadian Psychiatric Association Journal*, Sharon Shalev similarly noted how the "decline [in brain activity] was correlated with apathetic, lethargic behavior. Up to seven days the EEG decline is reversible, but if deprived over a long period this may not be the case" (Shalev,2008:p.20; citing Scott and Gendreau,1969).

According to University of Michigan neuroscientist Huda Akil, keeping people isolated for extended periods of time like this ruins "a very critical component of the brain that's sensitive to stress" (Stromberg, 2014). She posits that prolonged isolation, and the accompanying stress and depression may be dramatically shrinking the part of the brain used in memory, decision-making, and more (Ibid.).

So, here we have conditions that actually alter a person's brain - the most important organ of the body - and affects their ability to function normally, and most states in the U.S., as well as the federal government and President, are seemingly okay with this fact. This is curious when one considers that any physical, rather than mental, damage done to a person's body by an agent of the state - i.e. a bruise, a bloody nose, a broken rib - is actionable in court. However, the destruction of a person's mind by the State is not only "not torture" according to the President, but thanks to the Prison Litigation Reform Act (PLRA), nor is it actionable in court. The PLRA requires that a prisoner show physical harm. Mental or emotional harm is not considered serious enough to a warrant a court's intervention, let alone monetary damages.

The effects on the minds of juveniles are even worse. They suffer these symptoms in the midst of a crucial period in brain development. "Research shows that solitary confinement can do lasting damage to kids' brains. Yet dozens of states still routinely punish juveniles with days or weeks in the hole" (Liebelson, 2015:p.48). Compared to the years and decades adults are spending in isolation that may not seem like a long time, but the possibility of severely altering a child's life-course needs to be taken extremely serious. There are over 2,000 juvenile facilities in the U.S. and around 20% use isolation (Ibid:p.50-51). How many kids in those 400 or so facilities have experienced a cosmic shift from being rehabilitated to being mentally or criminally ill, by being arbitrarily thrown in isolation for a few weeks because staff didn't feel like dealing with them? We'll never know.

The most convincing way to demonstrate that prolonged isolation has detrimental mental health effects is to experience it for oneself. You'd be hard-pressed to find anyone who has spent years in solitary confinement who will honestly say that it did not affect them.

One inmate - who was also a victim of physical torture prior to arrest at the hands of notorious Chicago Police Lieutenant Jon Burge - found himself in Illinois' Tamms Supermax Prison. He described it as follows: "Tamms is a hell-hole. It is not a place for humans. Tamms was made to break you mentally, physically, and spiritually, in every detail of its operation" (Eisenman and Reynolds, 2009). Another inmate at Tamms who was housed on an elevated security wing has said:

> I feel like I am disintegrating. The isolation has affected
> my mind. It is like your head is in a vice, with pressure
> crushing you. You are isolated from everything that
> made you who you are. I am coming apart. I can't
> connect. It's psychological torture. Tamms is worse
> than any other place I have been because of the
> depersonalization you go through. The sensory
> deprivation eats away at your soul. You are not able to
> interact with another human being (Szilak, 2012:p.21).

Brian Nelson, who also spent many years at Tamms, calls it "a tomb....
[s]itting in a gray box all day, you just give up" (Keyser, 2012).The
Angola Three - Robert Hillary King, Herman Wallace, and Albert
Woodfox - have each spent decades in solitary confinement in the
Louisiana State Penitentiary at Angola for allegedly killing a prison
guard. King was released from prison in 2001 after spending 29 years
in solitary confinement. In his autobiography he writes,"[s]olitary
confinement is terrifying, especially if you are innocent of the charges
that put you there. It evokes a lot of emotion. It was a nightmare. My
soul still cries from all I witnessed and endured....There's no
describing the day to day assault on your body and your mind and the
feelings of helplessness and despair" (as cited in Friedmann,2012:p.4).

The other two of the Angola Three - Wallace and Woodfox - were not
fortunate enough to be released. They have remained isolated for over
four decades now (Ridgeway and Casella, 2011:p.4; Friedmann,
2012:p.5). *Solitary Watch* reported that the three of them "were
targeted for the crime because of their membership in a chapter of the
Black Panthers.... Both [Wallace and Woodfox] are now in their 60s,
but the warden maintains they must be kept in isolation because they
are 'still trying to practice Black Pantherism' and he does not want to
'have the blacks chasing after them' (Ridgeway and Casella,2011:p.4).

Wilbert Rideau also found himself in Angola in solitary confinement,

25

but on death row. In his memoir, *In The Place Of Justice*, Rideau describes the "bone-cold loneliness"of it:

> Removed from family or anything resembling a friend, and just being there with no purpose or meaning to my life, cramped in a cage smaller than an American bathroom. The lonesomeness was only increased by the constant cacophony of men in adjacent cells hurling shouted insults, curses, and arguments - not to mention the occasional urine or feces concoction" (Ibid.).

On June 19, 2012, Anthony Graves testified before the U.S. Senate Committee on the Judiciary's Subcommittee on the Constitution, Civil Rights and Human Rights about his 12 years on death row in Texas.

> Like all death row inmates, I was kept in solitary confinement. I lived under some of the worst conditions imaginable with the filth, the food, the total disrespect of human dignity. I lived under the rules of a system that is literally driving men out of their minds.... Solitary confinement does one thing, it breaks a man's will to live and he ends up deteriorating. I have been free for almost two years and I still cry at night because no one out here can relate to what I have gone through. I battle with feelings of loneliness. I've tried therapy, but it didn't work. The therapist was crying more than me. She couldn't believe that our system was putting men through this sort of inhumane treatment (Friedmann, 2012:p.4).

Graves was exonerated in 2010 after 18 years of being falsely convicted (Ibid.).

Sarah Jo Prender has seen plenty during her years in isolation. She was thrown in solitary confinement in Indiana in retaliation for successfully escaping prison in 2008 (Law, 2014:p.12). She conveyed to *Prison Legal News* that she "watched a woman claw chunks out of her cheeks and nose and write on the window with her blood";and how her "neighbor bashed her head against the concrete until officers dragged her out to a padded cell. Two other women tried to asphyxiate themselves with shoestrings and bras" (Ibid:p.13). None of them, including Prender, had preexisting mental health conditions prior to being isolated (Ibid:p.13). Nevertheless, by 2010, Prender herself experienced a 9-month psychotic break and now needs psychotropic medications (Ibid:p.13).

The state prison systems aren't the only ones putting people through this torture either. The Federal Bureau of Prisons is just as guilty. Their longest solitary confined inmate is Thomas "Tommy" Silverstein. He has been held under a "no human contact" order for 30 years (Friedmann, 2012:p.4). Pushing 60, he has had an immaculate disciplinary record for over twenty years (Burnett, 2011), and describes solitary as "a slow, constant peeling of the skin" (Friedmann, 2012:p.11).

People who have experienced both prolonged solitary confinement and physical torture come away fearing the former more than the latter. For instance, a member of the Tupamaro Movement[1] in Uruguay who experienced both said, "electricity [torture] is mere child's play in comparison to prolonged solitude" (Shalev, 2008 : p. 18 ; citing Reyes , 2007 : p. 607).

Society though, is quick to write off all prisoners, "Ex-cons", and revolutionaries as not being credible or just plain liars. So, when there is no visible harm and just the victim's word that he suffered mental harm, society is more inclined to believe that mental health

---

[1] The Tupamaro Movement was a Marxist guerilla group in Uruguay. In 1973, a repressive military regime took over the government to try to suppress them. For years, Tupamaro members were confined, isolated and tortured. In 2010, though, a former Tupamaro guerilla, Jose (Pepe) Mujica became president of Uruguay (Shalev, 2008:p.18; The World Alamanac, 2011:p.849).

deterioration due to isolation is fabricated. But what about when those former prisoners are also well-respected world leaders and dignitaries?

Nobel Laureate Nelson Mandela explained in his book *The Long Walk To Freedom*, how he "found solitary confinement the most forbidding aspect of prison life. There is no end and no beginning; there is only one's mind, which can begin to play tricks. Was that a dream or did it really happen? One begins to question everything" (as quoted in Shalev, 2003:p.18). Nor is it just liberals who will admit that mental anguish can amount to torture. Senator and former Republican Presidential Nominee, John McCain was a P.O.W. during the Vietnam War and experienced both isolation and physical torture. He has said that the isolation and accompanying mental torment was worse than the physical torture he endured (Eberhardt and Theoharis, 2011:p.9). "It's an awful thing, solitary. It crushes your spirit and weakens your resistance more effectively than any other form of mistreatment" (Friedmann, 2012:p.1; citing Kozar, 2001).

The decline in mental health eventually manifests itself into a variety of threats toward the inmate's physical self. It has long been known that symptoms resulting from isolation are "likely to mature into either homicidal or suicidal behavior" (Shalev, 2008:p.20; quoting McCleery, 1961: p. 265). Or, as Bob Corliss of the National Alliance on Mental Illness explained, "[t]hey become a greater risk to harm themselves and somebody else" (Isaacs and Lowen, 2007:p.18; citing Matthews, 2006).

As these symptoms often lead to violent outbursts, the inmate will suffer whether the outburst is directed at himself or others. As Sharon Shalev explains, "violent outbursts... turned upon the prisoner himself [come in two forms] self harm or suicide" (Shalev, 2008:p.20). Inmates may begin any of a number of self-destructive behaviors. Some will simply do things that are dangerous but not physically painful, such as swallowing finger-nail clippers or inserting ink pen tubes in their urethras. The danger to their physical safety is then compounded by the necessity of having surgery to extract the foreign object.

Many more though, punch or slam their heads against the cement walls or steel doors out of pure frustration, or become "cutters" to "feel alive." Cutters is the name prisoners give to those who cut themselves. In Tamms, inmates had bitten or cut off whole chunks of flesh. On more than one occasion, they've then eaten the chunk of flesh in front of staff.

The John Howard Association reported on this phenomenon in 2012 after touring Tamms:

> Inmates spoke of cutting and self-mutilation as ways to relieve a buildup of pressure and to feel "real" again. An inmate, who currently was not cutting but had deep scars from prior acts of self-mutilation, described to JHA that there was a vicious circle in that when he engaged in self-harm, his cell would be stripped of property, leaving him more deprived and causing the pressure to build again.
>
> JHA also received numerous reports from inmates of being disciplined and penalized for acts of self-harm...
>
> JHA believes that attaching punitive sanctions to acts of self-harm and stigmatizing those who self-harm as "manipulative" is unreasonable and counterproductive where these behaviors are typically symptomatic of mental distress and mental illness brought on by long-term isolation (Szilak, 2012:p.18-19).

One of those Tamms cutters almost completely severed his penis on numerous occasions. He repeatedly tried to castrate himself as well. On separate occasions, he finally succeeded in cutting off both his penis (which was later reattached at the hospital) and removing a testicle (which was not). Mental Health staff would often tell other inmates at Tamms that he "isn't crazy, he just wants attention." One would think that a mental health professional of any real caliber would, at the very least, have the common sense to realize that if someone is trying to castrate himself for attention, then he is clearly severely mentally ill or "crazy".

More often than not though, the mental health staff employed to work in control units and supermax prisons are not sincerely interested in treating or helping the inmates. Instead, they are mostly there as a bulwark against lawsuits filed by, or on behalf of, prisoners. Mental health personnel that have a strong conscience or moral compass usually either quit soon after starting, or are fired when they fail to provide cover for the inhumane policies implemented by the prison administration.

Former Tamms inmate Brian Nelson claimed confinement there was causing him to have "persistent suicidal thoughts for the first time in his life" (Tietz, 2012:p.63). A court ordered "psychiatrist recommended that he be removed from solitary immediately" (ibid.). That recommendation was ignored by prison administrators (Ibid.) who had their own psychiatrist who said he was fine. He went on to try to kill himself twice, one of which times they found him "in his cell with rope burns around his neck" (Keyser, 2012a).

While suicides are not exclusive to control units and supermaxes, they are much more prevalent due to the more intense deterioration of the population's mental health there. It is commonly reported that, nationally, half of all suicides are committed in solitary confinement (Kupers and Moltz, 2010; Ridgeway and Casella,2012; *Harper's Magazine*, 2012:p.13) . Isaacs and Lowen's Summary of Key Findings tells how, "supermax confinement increases the risk of prisoner suicides. New York State found that 53 percent of all mentally ill inmates in supermax confinement had attempted suicide" (Isaacs and Lowen, 2007:p.5). It may be even higher though, *Solitary Watch* reported that "studies have found that two-thirds of all prison suicides take place in solitary confinement" (*Solitary Watch* Newsletter, 2011:p.3). In 2006, 69% of suicides in California, the largest prison system in the country, were committed in isolation cells (Magnani, 2008:p.9), and in 2007, 67% were (Ibid:p.12). With as little as two percent, and, at most, 10% of the prison population in solitary confinement, it is telling that between 50% and 69% of suicides happen in control units, supermaxes, and other isolation chambers.

Sadly, juveniles are also at an increased risk of suicide if subjected to isolation, which we've seen they routinely are. Over a five-year period 79 kids killed themselves in juvenile facilities (Liebelson, 2015:p.52). Sixty-two percent of them had spent time isolated, "and more than half took their lives while they were in 'room confinement'" (Ibid.).

There have even been prisoners who were facing a lifetime of solitary confinement that have asked judges for a death sentence instead (Ridgeway and Casella, 2011:p.4). This is a twisted version of the old "death by cop," where someone who can't bring themselves to commit suicide tries to force the police to kill him or her instead. Here though, it's "death by judge", and they're literally begging to be put out of their misery. Conditions that push people to beg for death or take their own lives in order to escape them, can only be seen as the epitome of inhumane.

When an inmate's rage is turned on others, it also poses a serious threat to his or her own safety as well. Trying to assault staff while in a control unit or supermax will likely result in being maced and then violently assaulted in retaliation (often after being handcuffed and defenseless). The same result will likely occur if the assault on staff takes place once they are released into general population. Similarly, if he or she assaults another inmate in general population it may result in him or her being physically harmed in the altercation. This may be at the hands of the other inmate, by responding staff, or both.

Often inmates don't even need to assault staff in these units to be abused by staff. The fact that inmates have few opportunities to seriously harm staff in supermaxes gives staff an enhanced feeling of security. In a normal prison environment, most staff will refrain from openly abusing inmates out of fear of retaliation either by that inmate or by his or her friends or fellow gang members. It is one of the few checks and balances that inmates still retain. In a supermax though, with inmates behind a steel door the majority of the time, staff feel safe from attack or retaliation. This also makes them feel free to attack, because they are almost assured not to suffer any repercussions. This is why "power trips" by guards are not only much more extreme and prolonged in supermaxes, but also why they occur much more frequently than in general population.

It's like a little kid poking a bear with a stick through the bars at a zoo or circus. They feel invincible. Even more above the law than usual. Some staff routinely mistreat inmates, violating their constitutional rights and arbitrarily antagonizing them for sport. So just being in a supermax greatly increases the risk that an inmate will be abused by staff. With the injustices piling up and the prison grievance system and courts arbitrarily dismissing most prisoner complaints, inmates become angrier, more frustrated, hate-filled, and volatile.

These isolation units also pose a threat of increased prison time to those confined to them. This can come about through a variety of ways. As the Istanbul Statement on the Use and Effects of Solitary Confinement notes, the detrimental effects will often create a de facto situation of psychological pressure which can influence the pretrial detainees to plead guilty" (Istanbul Statement, 2007:p.64). It isn't just pretrial detainees though that are being coerced. A common practice of the supermax prisons and control units is to try and force inmates into renouncing gang membership and snitching on other inmates in order to win a transfer out of isolation. Renouncing usually requires answering questions concerning one's past criminal activities, as well as what one knows about the criminal activities of others. The inmate's interrogation is videotaped and can be used against him or her later in a court of law.

These renunciation policies are "typically known as 'snitch.., parole, or die' policies" (Friedmann, 2012:p.7; citing *Solitary Watch*'s website). Snitching on oneself means being charged with new criminal cases. Snitching on others in prison means that the inmate is now at risk of being physically assaulted in retaliation for snitching; something he or she may not have done without being coerced by years of inhumane treatment and the hope of an end to the isolation.

Often, mentally ill inmates with just a few years remaining on their sentences will be transferred to a supermax or control unit, and will catch so many new charges before their release date that they accumulate new sentences to the point they serve a de facto life sentence. A common charge is assaulting a guard or other staff member by hurling blood, urine, or feces at them. The conviction in criminal court can add another five years to one's sentence in Illinois. For someone who is mentally unstable, frustrated, and constantly abused, this behavior may repeat itself on a daily basis. Thus, the sentences can quickly add up to 50, 100, or more years being tacked on to one's sentence. Even if they dodge that bullet and are released, their symptoms and time in a supermax increases their likelihood of recidivating (committing a new crime and being reincarcerated).

More than anything though, these places threaten to destroy one's humanity. Treat people inhumanely long enough and there's a good chance they will cease to care about others and treat others in a similar vein - with total disregard for their feelings, interests, rights, or safety.

Suicide, self-mutilation, being victimized by devices of torture, and as-saulted by guards aren't the only physical harm that those in supermaxes and other control units are vulnerable to. Just being there for an extended period of time damages one's physical health.

Although the amount of research done on the physical or physiological effects of long-term solitary confinement is negligible compared to that done on the mental health effects, what's out there leaves little doubt that such conditions do result in adverse effects to a person's body as well as his or her mind. (In addition to quite possibly shrinking one's brain.).

As already mentioned, increased stress and anxiety are pervasive there. Both of these are known to cause cardiovascular problems such as high blood pressure, heart palpitations, etc. Doctors have long noted that stress causes harm to both the mind and body and can shave years off of one's life.

When Sharon Shalev reviewed the various studies on the effects of solitary confinement when compiling her *Sourcebook*, she found that "physiological effects are... commonly reported. Some of these may be physical manifestations of psychological stress, but the lack of access to fresh air and sunlight and long periods of inactivity are likely to have physical consequences" (Shalev, 2008:p.15). She lists a number of these effects and consequences: gastrointestinal, cardiovascular, and genitourinary problems; migraine headaches; profound fatigue; diaphoresis (sudden excessive sweating); insomnia; back and other joint pains; deterioration of eyesight; poor appetite, weight loss, and sometimes diarrhea; lethargy; weakness; tremulousness (shaking); feeling cold; and aggravation of pre-existing medical problems (Shalev,2008:p.15 ; citing Grassian and Friedmann, 1986; and Korn, 1988). *Solitary Watch* reported in 2011 that:

> Evidence from recent court cases suggests a relationship to things like extreme insomnia, joint pain, hypertension and even damage to the eyesight which

> makes sense when you are talking about not being able
> to walk or look more than ten feet in any direction for
> years on end. We will clearly see more evidence of
> health damage as more and more prisoners grow old in
> long-term solitary confinement (*Solitary Watch
> Newsletter*, 2011:p.3).

Any distance runner can tell you that running on concrete is punishing
to one's heels, ankles, knees, and lower back. Prisoners in supermaxes
are usually denied access to shoes with any real cushion or arch
support. Often they are only allowed canvas shoes with cardboard
soles. Inmates have very few options to exercise - the most common
being... running on concrete. Even if they choose not to, it will matter
little because they live on concrete 24-7, never feeling the comfort of
carpet or grass. The human body did not evolve to withstand the
rigorous pounding that living on concrete entails.

It is also common knowledge that loud noises deteriorate one's hearing
and cause stress. Hence, people wear earplugs when working in
factories and other loud workplaces; and build two-story high, noise-
deadening walls along highways that pass too close to residential
areas. At Tamms and many other supermax prisons and control units,
earplugs were, or are, verboten.

The constant slamming of steel on steel as chuckholes and cell doors
are slammed opened and closed hundreds of times per day for years on
end damages hearing and induces stress. Yelling also induces stress,
and is usually the only form of communication an inmate has with his
or her neighbors. The yelling and the steel din constantly shatter an
otherwise silent environment. Even *Rolling Stone* has reported on
these phenomena:

> The concrete environment refracts noise many times
> over: It can be hard to identify the source of a sound,
> refracted and muddled and sustained by echoes...the
> ambient volume fluctuates wildly, swinging from sonic

chaos to silence and back... [and] over time, the visual monotony and erratic acoustics become fatiguing and neurologically unsettling. Many inmates experience a degeneration of distance vision. They are rarely more than a dozen feet from a wall and with nothing far off to focus on, their eye muscles atrophy (Tietz, 2012:p.64).

Therefore, the threats that solitary confinement pose to an inmate's mind and body are not only very real, but significant and even life-threatening. Even if they don't shorten an inmate's life, they will almost certainly cause the inmate's quality of life both inside and outside of prison to deteriorate.

-THREAT TO STAFF-

Since these units fail to rehabilitate prisoners and actually make them less mentally stable and often more violent, when they are released back into the general population of prisons - as many eventually are - they pose an increased threat to staff. This fact shouldn't be hard to comprehend. As we've already seen, one of the side effects of prolonged isolation is irrational anger. That irrational anger is just as likely to manifest itself in violence against staff members as it is against other inmates. Prison guards know this, it's one reason why they fight so vociferously against supermax closures. The solution isn't to continue treating inmates inhumanely though; it is to stop putting them in these units and making them irrationally angry in the first place.

The John Howard Association notes how: "To date there is no evidence that Tamms or supermax prisons in general achieve the goal of reducing violence or improving system-wide order and safety. Indeed, there is evidence to the contrary that supermax prisons increase institutional violence and rates of violent recidivism" (Szilak, 2012:p.5). In compiling her *Sourcebook*, Shalev found that, "studies identified isolation regimes as central factors leading to prison riots. One study of events leading to the 1980 riot in the New Mexico Penitentiary (USA), for example, attributed the riot directly to the strategy of isolating prisoner leaders, which led to the fragmentation of prisoner solidarity and in turn led to growing violence" (Shalev, 2008:p.32).

Both Columbia and Mexico are very familiar with this phenomenon. In Columbia, the Medellin drug cartel was headed by Pablo Escobar who was killed in 1993. As Sara Reardon notes in *New Scientist*, "like a hydra, chopping off the head only caused the cartel to splinter into smaller networks... which tend to assert their power by torturing and killing people" (Reardon, 2012). Three years later, Columbia had 300 "baby cartels which are still powerful today" (Ibid.).

Not too long ago, Mexico only had a couple major drug cartels which, for the most part, co-existed peacefully just happy to make a lot of money. Once the heads of the cartels were taken out though, the cartels started splintering, fighting for control over different areas, and branching into mass murder and kidnapping for ransom. As they became more violent fighting each other, they also became more violent with the public, press, and police. Recent policy has been to increasingly target the heads of cartels. This doesn't seem to be working. "Prior to the [government] crackdowns that began in 2006, drug-related crimes in Mexico killed about 3,700 people per year. In 2011, that number was more than 16,000" (Reardon, 2012).

Likewise, increased prison violence doesn't seclude itself within the prisoner population. Donald Cabana, a former Mississippi prison warden, says that the supermax environment "actually increases the level of hostility and anger among inmates and staff alike" (Gibbons and de B. Katzenbach, 2006 p.54).

In other words, supermax prisons and control units poison all involved, not just those who are isolated within them, but those who oversee their isolation as well. Just working in them can have serious repercussions. Dr. Lorne A. Rhodes reported in the *American Journal of Public Health* that:

> Consequences also extend to the staff of these prisons, many from rural towns, who learn a numbingly mechanistic, impersonal, and potentially brutalizing form of work. Some prison workers are able to resist these effects, but many develop a punitive attitude that eventually affect their families and communities (Rhodes, 2005:p.1695).

Prison Legal News reported that correctional workers in American prisons in general have a life expectancy of only 59 years due to the damage caused "by performing purely punitive functions" and all of the accompanying "stress, hypertension, alcoholism, suicide, and other job-related hazards" (Larson, 2014). So, the increase of those factors in a control unit or supermax prison, which is even more punitive and forces them to also deal with the severely mentally ill as well, cannot be good for the already shortened life expectancy of staff working there.

Correctional officers working in Pelican Bay State Prison (which houses 1056 people in harsh conditions of solitary confinement (Shalev, 2008:p.48)) admitted that rates of alcoholism, spousal abuse, and suicide had skyrocketed among them (Kamel and Kerness, 2003:p.7). Dr. Stuart Grassian, after speaking with them, reported that "over time [working there] destroys you psychologically and brings out rage and sadism and violence and brutality" (Ibid.). The American Friends Service Committee (AFSC) of Philadelphia noted succinctly that, "[b]rutality - [guards] have learned, inevitably rebounds on those who practice it" (Ibid.).

The magazine *Odyssey* reported on this nearly two decades ago:

> Don Houseworth, a psychologist and former deputy director of Michigan corrections, warns of the dangers to prison guards. They begin to lose all empathy for the prisoners. "If you prepare a guard consistently to be on the lookout for violence, and if you describe the prisoner in non-human terms," he says[sic]. The process of dehumanizing others is a common psychological defense that enables prison guards to commit brutal acts against prisoners without suffering guilt.
>
> But dehumanizing others affects one's own humanity. It is not surprising that stress and alcohol and drug abuse are so high among prison guards who work in these maximum security environments. Burn out is common

and many of the guards have marital problems. One state Director of Corrections said about Control Units, "In this kind of atmosphere it becomes possible to think of abuse as normal, and if you are not careful you have a staff out of control" (O'Shea, 1993:p.42).

Ten years later, the AFSC would likewise note that, "[t]his culture of violence is profoundly destructive to those who suffer its effects, brutalizing not only prisoners, but also prison guards and officials who become daily agents of inhumanity" (Kamel and Kerness, 2003:p.12). So it's not just the prisoners (who are repeatedly, and falsely, labeled the "worst of the worst") who are victims of prolonged solitary confinement. So too are those who work inside the control units and supermaxes. Prison guards' unions often ignore this fact and think only of the added positions and higher pay of supermax or control unit positions when they claim that these places are necessary as the only means to keep violence down and staff everywhere safe. A theory that has now been completely debunked.

It is also a myth that guards working in isolation units are safe. Although it may be harder for inmates in supermaxes or control units to assault prison guards, it is not impossible. Treat a person inhumanely long enough and he or she will figure out a way to retaliate.

That is what happened with one ex-Tamms inmate. One of the last inmates to leave Tamms, the unidentified 53-year old was transferred to a control unit in Pontiac Correctional Center. When a tactical team rushed in his cell for refusing to cuff-up, the inmate retreated under his bunk and used a homemade knife to attack the weak spots in the guards' armor. He successfully stabbed three guards numerous times in the hands, legs, forearms, and wrists, sending them all to the hospital (O'Connor, 2015).

-THREAT TO SOCIETY-

Far from providing enhanced security to society, these facilities are actually a national security threat. They severely threaten the public in a plethora of ways. Probably the most easily deducible of which is the monetary costs borne by society.

Supermax prisons are incredibly expensive both in their construction and operation. The federal ADX Florence facility cost $60 million to build; Tamms cost $73 million; and Pelican Bay cost $230 million. That comes out to $122,000, $146,000, and $217,000 per bed respectively (Friedmann, 2012:p.9). While tha average cost of building a medium security prison bed would cost about $65,000 per bed (Ibid.).

Operating them eats up taxpayer dollars at an accelerated rate as well. Ohio's supermax chews through $149 per prisoner per day, compared to $63 if he were in general population (Ibid.). Arizona spends about $50,000 per year to isolate an inmate compared to $20,000 for non-isolated prisoners (Ibid.). The Illinois Department of Corrections (IDOC) claimed that it spent $64,805 per prisoner per year to seal an inmate in Tamms (Szilak, 2012:p.2), which is nearly three times the $22,043 average (Friedmann,2012:p.9). The IDOC used creative accounting though to hide the true costs from the public. It actually cost Illinois taxpayers four times as much to house an inmate in Tamms - or $92,000 per year (Pawlacyzyk and Hundsdorfer, 2009b).

The worrisome irony is that all of this added expense does not contribute to public safety in any way. Instead it does the opposite. As we've already seen, overall the conditions make both staff and inmates alike more violent. Staff return to the community after each shift and most of the inmates will someday be released. The additional money appropriated for these prisoners is not spent on mitigating the threat posed by these now irrationally angry people being released. Rather than spending money to rehabilitate these prisoners or treat their mental health problems so that they pose less of a threat to society, these prisons and units are designed with no space devoted to educational or rehabilitative programming, and routinely deny both medical and mental health care to their populations. The added expense is used for concrete and steel, dozens, if not hundreds of surveillance cameras, monitors, and other high-tech gadgetry, as well as an abundance of overpaid staff.

Writing about supermaxes in the early 1990s, Patrick O'Shea concluded that they "are the most expensive illusions to security that public money can buy" (O'Shea, 1993:p.43). It is even more illusory now after an extended recession where state governments are in such dire straits that they are now forced to lay off thousands of teachers, police officers, and fire fighters due to lack of funds. The funds drained away by supermaxes and other isolation units could actually be doing what the myth of supermaxes and other isolation units claims to do - help to maintain institutional security and keep society safe.

That money could be better spent on programs to rehabilitate inmates; keep police officers on the street to prevent crime; make police accountable for their misconduct to reduce wrongful convictions and the frequency with which citizens are harassed at taxpayer expense; employ sufficient firefighters to save both additional lives and property; and employ more teachers ensuring that the next generation is literate, educated, and possesses marketable skill sets reducing the likelihood they will resort to a life of crime.

Some states are beginning to recognize that supermaxes are not just unaffordable and counterproductive, but actively draining away limited funds from deprived social services. As a result, they are closing them. Mississippi sees an annual $5.5 million in savings since 2010 due to closing Unit 32 at Parchman State Penitentiary (Friedmann,2012:p.9-10). Former Illinois Governor Pat Quinn reckoned that closing Tamms would save Taxpayers nearly $22 million per year (Ibid.:p.l0). When State legislators tried to appropriate $50 million to turn Tamms into a medium security facility, Quinn refused and redirected the funds to the Department of Child and Family Services which was severely underfunded.

Unfortunately, not all states were paying attention. Colorado, "with deep budget cuts to education and social services... opened up 300 additional solitary confinement cells" (CFPR,2010b), and, as we'll see later on, had to reverse course shortly thereafter.

Also, the John Howard Association noted,"[t]here is growing recognition across the country that the supermax model is proving to be of questionable efficacy, prohibitively expensive to maintain, and a source of continuous litigation" (Szilak, 2012:p.25). The amount of litigation that comes out of control units and supermax prisons is incomparable to other prisons. This is another significant cost to taxpayers that is never factored into operating costs. Lawsuits filed by prisoners housed in these places are filed in desperation, usually without counsel, and with inadequate knowledge of the law. Nevertheless, they are filed in an attempt to protect their constitutional rights and to try to obtain a transfer out of isolation.

According to the Associated Press, these types of cases "are coming with increasing regularity" (Associated Press, 2012). "A Federal jury in January [2012] awarded $22 million to a New Mexico inmate who extracted a tooth by hand, rocking it back and forth in the socket for hours, after going without medical or dental care while in solitary confinement for two years" (Ibid.). Ernesto Lira, a California prisoner who was wrongfully validated as a gang member and tossed in isolation for 8 years was awarded $1 million in attorney fees after a four-week trial in which the Court found that he suffered from both clinical depression and PTSD as a result (Friedmann, 2012:p.6) .

A four-week long trial could not have been cheap. That's probably more than a twelfth of that courtroom's docket time for the year. Nor will the mental health care that he'll require to overcome the damage his isolation caused be cheap. All of the mental and medical care that is denied to inmates while in supermaxes will all be borne by society sooner or later. Emergency medical care while in supermaxes is not cheap either. So when inmates are denied proper preventative care and it turns into an emergency situation the cost is much greater.

Then there's the emergency care required due to self-harm because inmates are denied proper mental health care. A trip to an outside hospital to remove ink pens from an inmate's urethra cost the State of Illinois over $10,000 per trip. Or, as the John Howard Association noted,"[s]elf-harming behavior is extremely costly in terms of both danger and damage to inmates and the facility resources required for intervention" (Szilak, 2012:p.19). So too will society have to bear the added costs when these inmates can't keep a job or find employment due to their untreated mental health issues, and it necessitates an increased use of social welfare programs.

Furthermore, as we'll see below, these isolation units also cause those prisoners who are released from them straight to the streets to have higher recidivism rates. Increased crime equals increased costs to society - additional insurance costs and hospital bills of victims; costs of additional police responses; additional criminal court proceedings; and additional costs of incarceration; just to name a few.

All of these additional and unnecessary costs take away from the coffers of federal and state governments, compromising their ability to adequately fund rehabilitative programs, police forces, fire departments, schools, and more. As already noted, the conditions in these units engender hatred and irrational anger in those who survive them. It should come as no surprise then, that rather than becoming less violent when released, the opposite occurs, and society pays the price.

A prime example of this was Evan Ebel. A young man serving an eight-year sentence in Colorado for a 2005 carjacking, Ebel had behavioral problems as a child. These turned into criminal activity and then a prison sentence. Instead of receiving adequate mental health care, he was tossed into isolation. He spent nearly his entire sentence there, and his mental illness severely worsened (Dannenberg, 2014:p.1-3).

Prior to release, Ebel had asked the prison administration in a grievance, "Do you have any obligation to the public to reacclimate me, the dangerous inmate, to being around other human beings prior to being released, and, if not, why?" (Ibid.:p.4). The written response he received was that a grievance was not the appropriate place to discuss policy (lbid.:p.4). The real, but unwritten, answer was a definitive indifference, which was clearly evident by Ebel's release straight to the streets from solitary confinement on January 23, 2013 (lbid.:p.4).

Within two months, Ebel cut off his ankle monitor, killed two people, and was himself killed. First, he abducted a pizza delivery man on March 17, 2013, and forced him to read the following statement into a tape recorder:

> [Y]ou didn't give two shits about us or our families and you ensured that we were locked behind a door, to disrespect us at every opportunity, so why should we care about you and yours[?]...In short, you treated us inhumanely, and we simply seek to do the same, we take [comfort] in the knowledge that we leave your wives without husbands, and your children fatherless. You wanted to play the mad scientist, well they [prisoners held in solitary] will be your Frankenstein (lbid.:p.l).

Ebel then shot and killed the deliveryman and took his uniform (Ibid.:p.l). He wore it two days later to belay suspicion when he knocked on Colorado Department of Corrections Director Tom Clements' door. Clements answered the door and Ebel shot him at point-blank-range, leaving him to die in his wife's arms (Ibid.:p.l).

Two days after that, Deputy James Boyd would receive several gunshot wounds when he pulled Eben over for a traffic violation in Texas. This led to a police chase ending in a shootout where Ebel was shot dead on March 21, 2013 (Ibid.:p.1) .

This episode has brought a lot of attention to the problems of releasing people back to the streets directly from solitary confinement in Colorado. While bringing "systemic changes" there, according to *Prison Legal News*, it has brought zero acknowledgement that solitary confinement was the catalyst of Ebel's actions (Ibid.:p.l,4).

A decade earlier, in *The Prison Inside the Prison: Control Units, Supermax Prisons, and Devices of Torture*, Rachel Kamel and Bonnie Kerness noted that, "[i]t is well documented that sustained isolation and sensory deprivation leave many prisoners overwhelmed with rage and paranoia that they are unable to understand or control" (Kamel and Kerness,2003:p.8). They quote Stuart Grassian who said:

> It's kind of like kicking and beating a dog and keeping it in a cage until it gets as crazy and vicious and wild as it can possibly get and then one day you take it out into the middle of the streets of San Francisco or Boston and you open the cage and you run away. That's no favor to the community (Ibid.).

The John Howard Association had similarly noted that "there is evidence... that supermax prisons increase... rates of recidivism. This...fact is particularly troubling, given that the majority of Tamms inmates will be released and returned to the community" (Szilak, 2012:p.5). Likewise, the MacArthur Justice Center alleged in a lawsuit on behalf of mentally ill prisoners at Tamms, that their inhumane treatment "harms society as well as th[o]se prisoners...[who] will return to the streets sicker, angrier, and more violent" (FeIshman,2008).

All of this has been known for quite a while. Sharon Shalev noted that, "[a] study of the 'incorrigible units' in North Carolina in the late 1950s, where prisoners were subjected to a regime of strict and prolonged solitary confinement, concluded that 'the overall impact of the incorrigible unit in penal practice probably is one that intensifies tendencies to criminal attitude and behavior'" (Shalev, 2008:p.32, citing McCleery, 1981:p.306).

Unfortunately, most states and the federal government seem content with the status quo. They refuse to acknowledge a problem and deliberately keep the public ignorant about how large a threat supermaxes pose to society. This is evident by the fact that they largely refuse to even study what the recidivism rates are for solitary confinement releasees, let alone try to mitigate the problem. One of the few to even study it was Washington state. They studied 8,000 prisoners who were released in 1997 and 1998. The recidivism rate was 23% higher (64% compared to 41%) for prisoners released directly from segregation than from general population (Gibbons and de B. Katzenbach, 2006:p.55). By that measure, segregation prior to release makes a person more than 50% more likely to recidivate. When a reporter for *USA Today* tracked nine people who were released from "high-security segregation" in Texas, seven of them "had served additional time in prison" (Ibid.:p.52). That's a 78% recidivism rate.

There are many reasons why inmates released directly from supermax prisons have a higher recidivism rate than general population inmates (besides the fact that these prisons and units are incubators of hate). Nearly all of which can be directly attributed to the conditions they endured in long-term isolation.

At first glance, one would think that it is because the "worst of the worst" are sent there to begin with, and the "worst" would have higher recidivism rates regardless. As already shown though, it is rarely the "worst" criminals who are sent there. Also, counter-intuitively, violent criminals - the ones everyone always labels as the "worst" - have lower recidivism rates than non-violent criminals. Murderers actually have the lowest recidivism rates of any class of offenders. So, if only the "worst of the worst" (i.e. murderers) were sent to supermaxes and supermaxes didn't increases recidivism, then you would have lower recidivism rates for supermax releasees than for general population releasees.

Unfortunately, that's not what we see. Instead, we see higher recidivism rates. Part of the problem is that supermaxes, etc. are being crammed with mentally ill people, making them more ill, and even driving mentally healthy people, mentally ill, all while denying everyone adequate mental health treatment.

The American Friends Service Committee-Arizona (AFSC-Arizona) asked a poignant question that most correctional agencies are seemingly indifferent about answering - "Why would authorities release these [mentally ill] prisoners from solitary confinement to the community with no transitional time or assistance?" (Isaacs and Lowen, 2007:p.22). The threat posed by driving prisoners insane, or more insane, and then releasing them on society should be self-evident, and correctional agencies should take measures to mitigate that threat. This almost never happens though.

Additionally, supermaxes and control units knowingly work against the main goal of "corrections" - to rehabilitate offenders so that they cease to pose a threat to society. Correctional agencies view these units, first and foremost, as a place for punishment. Therefore, they are reluctant to grant inmates anything they consider to be a privilege. It is these "privileges" though, that are the most effective tools in reducing recidivism.

For instance, unlike the United Nations - which views education as a basic human right - correctional agencies in the United States see education as a privilege needing to be earned, and only offer it to select inmates. This is furthermore dependent on how many resources they are willing to allocate to educational courses. In supermaxes, which are for punishment not privileges, education is usually denied to inmates, and an inmate's attempts at self-education through books and correspondence courses are intentionally frustrated by the administration. Many of these units have severe limits on receiving publications, claim innocuous textbooks are a security threat, routinely "lose" mail, and either completely ban segregation inmates from enrolling in correspondence courses, or refuse to proctor exams. The latter two of which both mean that prisoners there can't work towards an actual college degree, but are instead left with non-accredited or bible study courses.

Likewise, vocational and re-entry programs are virtually non-existent. Most supermax prisons are intentionally designed and built without any space to offer programs. Prison jobs are also unheard of as there are no prison jobs able to be completed in one's cell. This deprives inmates of both work experience and the ability to save money in order to facilitate a smooth transition back into society when released.

There is universal agreement in the correctional industry that the most effective way to reduce recidivism is through education and/or vocational training. The Alabama State Board of Education concluded that "[c]orrectional education appears to be the number one factor in reducing recidivism rates nationwide" (Mosso,1997). It is therefore bewildering why the majority of supermaxes intentionally deny the "worst of the worst" any educational or re-entry programs. Shouldn't the priority be to rehabilitate these allegedly most dangerous inmates in order to protect society?

A common argument in favor of keeping "disruptive" inmates in prolonged isolation is that it allows the smooth functioning of operations in general population which allows for increased programs for non-isolated prisoners and reduces overall recidivism. There is no empirical data to support this theory though. Instead, what happens is that correctional agencies spend unconscionable amounts of money on supermaxes and control units and can no longer even afford the rehabilitative programs they had, let alone expand them. So, fewer inmates are rehabilitated instead of more, and the overall recidivism rate goes up.

This may be what occurred in Illinois. The IDOC opened Tamms in 1998. By 2000, all vocational courses had been completely abandoned in Menard Correctional Center, a maximum security prison housing over 3,000 inmates less than an hour's drive from Tamms. The overall recidivism rate in Illinois was 42.5 percent for the two years prior to Tamms opening (Friedmann,2012: p.8). "In the two years after the supermax opened the recidivism rates in Illinois increased by more than 28 percent...." (Ibid.). Tamms didn't even start allowing inmates to take the G.E.D. exam until 2010 after an intensive campaign by anti-supermax group Tamms Year Ten brought national attention to conditions at Tamms, forcing some small concessions by the IDOC administration.

By that year though, the John Howard Association would report both on the fact that college and vocational courses in Illinois prisons were rapidly disappearing (Manor and Maki,2010), and that inmates in all of the state's maximum security prisons were no longer being rehabilitated, but simply "warehoused" (Manor,2910a and 2010b). Thus, the opening of Tamms seems to have worked directly against the stated goal of imprisonment in Illinois - "to return offenders to useful citizenship" (Article 1, Section II of the Illinois Constitution; and 720 ILCS 5/l-l-2(b) and (d)).

Another factor which reduces one's likelihood of recidivating is maintaining close contact with his or her family and community. In supermaxes and control units - where mail is routinely delayed and/or confiscated for the most arbitrary reasons; where phone calls are often prohibited or too short and infrequent to be meaningful; and where visits are a hassle - this becomes nearly impossible.

Writing to the FCC concerning exorbitant prison phone rates, U.S. Representatives Bobby Rush and Henry Waxman stated that, "[r]esearch shows that regular contact between prisoners and families reduces recidivism. Phone calls are the primary means for families to maintain contact with incarcerated relatives" (Motel, 2012:p.20). Drew Kukorowski, writing in *Prison Legal News*, similarly reported that "family contact has been consistently shown to lower recidivism" (Kukorowski, 2012:p.20). He continued, "[i]ndeed the Federal Bureau of Prisons states that 'telephone privileges are a supplemental means of maintaining community and family ties that will contribute to an inmate's personal development'" (Ibid:p.21). Many supermax inmates though, either don't get to make any phone calls at all for years or decades prior to release, or get only one or two 10-15 minute phone calls per month.

When an inmate is in general population, not only can he or she maintain contact with their family through frequent phone calls, but just as importantly, they can get contact visits where they can hug their loved-ones, hold their children, share a meal, and converse normally. As Dr. Lorne A. Rhodes notes though:

> In the case of super maximum imprisonment, the consequences extend first to the families of prisoners, whose visits may be tightly restricted and who are allowed to see their imprisoned family members only through the thick plastic window of a visiting booth. Some long-term prisoners say that they do not want their families to see them under these circumstances... and gradually cut off contact" (Rhodes, 2005:p.1695).

The John Howard Association was adamant about the folly of policies that discourage visits:

> A frequent complaint heard from Tamms inmates and their family members is that rules, regulations, and procedures for scheduling visits are so burdensome, complicated, and exacting that they often frustrate visitation.... Inmates and family members expressed that the complicated hurdles to obtaining approval for visits, coupled with Tamms' geographic location, have caused most inmates to lose touch with their family and friends. Some inmates and family members reported having abandoned visiting altogether because of the harsh visiting environment, where inmates and family members sit on cement stools, separated by a glass wall, and communicate through voice-activated speakers .... Decades of research indicate that visits from family improve inmate's institutional behavior and lower the likelihood of recidivism. Despite this, policies and impediments that unduly discourage visitation prevail at Tamms.
>
> As stated in prior reports, JHA believes that creating policies and environments that encourage visitation should be a correctional priority. Inmates' families and friends, while routinely undervalued are, in fact, correctional assets, as studies show that visitation and communication between inmates and loved ones during incarceration reduces institutional violence and increases rates of post release success (Szilak, 2012:p.14-15).

Age is also a good indicator of the likelihood of recidivating. As prisoners age they mature and the majority of them will outgrow their criminal tendencies. Unfortunately, supermaxes retard this effect. As noted earlier, supermaxes cause inmates to regress. Even if the link to schizophrenia is not proven, common sense would suggest that if crime is mainly a pastime of the young and immature, then causing prisoners to regress to a more immature mentality cannot be good for one's likelihood of rehabilitation.

By frustrating an inmate's education and family/community ties, causing an inmate to regress to a more immature and crime-prone mindset, and increasing their rage and mental illnesses, the inmate is systematically being turned into more of a threat to society, not less.

Shalev (2008:p.22) notes how "[f]ormer prisoners who have spent prolonged periods in solitary confinement have testified to experiencing difficulties in social situations long after their release:

> My character and personality have undergone many negative changes and I am now a very paranoid and suspicious person. The paranoia has become so extensive that I find it impossible to trust anyone anymore and I have developed a tendency to hate people for no apparent reason" (Wakefield, 1980:p.30).

Professor Craig Haney calls these released prisoners "utterly dysfunctional when they get out" (Gibbons and de B. Katzenbach, 2006:p.52; citing Johnson, 2005). Some prisoners become so dependent on the strict daily routine of the supermax that they can't function in society because "they lose the capacity to exercise personal autonomy... and some will seek to return to prison" (Shalev, 2003:p.20). Obviously, that would entail committing another crime.

Furthermore, after years or decades of being denied any human contact or compassion of any kind, and completely isolated from society, it is unrealistic to expect someone released directly onto the streets from prolonged isolation, would behave as an upstanding citizen with the best interests of society in mind. After all, society just threw him or her into a virtual tomb and treated them in the most arbitrary and despicable manner without a second thought, nor a single care about how this affected him or her; so, why would he or she care about how their actions affect society? With ever-increasing concerns about domestic terrorism, one would think we would not actively try to turn our own citizens into people who hate society. Yet, all too often, that's exactly what supermaxes and control units are doing. Conversion to Muslim extremism was witnessed by this writer with much greater frequency in Tamms than in the general population of any maximum security prison in Illinois.

-GROWING ACKNOWLEDGMENT-

Many factors, including political pressure for harsh sentencing, the effect of unemployment in rural economies, population pressure inside prison systems, and the internal architectural and staffing features of general population units, influence the construction and use of supermaximum facilities across the country. Local administrators often have few options for reducing tension among prisoners, rewarding good behavior, or replacing disruptive or mentally ill prisoners. These issues, however, are seldom part of public debate about prisons and prison spending. Supermaximum prisons are generally off-limits to the public and the claim that they house the "worst of the worst" is rarely questioned in the press (Rhodes, 2005:p. 1692).

This all makes garnering opposition to, challenging, and dismantling supermaxes and control units incredibly difficult.

Until recently, it had mainly been human rights groups that have rung the warning bell about supermaxes and control units. Human Rights Watch warned nearly two decades ago that "[m]ost inmates in supermaximum security prisons will one day be released back into local communities. If these people have been abused, treated with violence, and confined in dehumanizing conditions that threaten their very mental health, they may well leave prison angry, dangerous and far less capable of leading law-abiding lives than when they entered" (Fellner and Mariner, 1997).

Ten years later, the AFSC-Arizona concluded that "[t]he long-term impacts of these policies reach far beyond the prison walls....the neglect and abuse festering within these units will ultimately find its way back to all of us in the form of broken families, higher incidences of mental illness, greater state spending on corrections at the expense of other needed programs, more assaults and disturbances, and, finally, *more* crime....AFSC views long-term solitary confinement as inappropriate, ineffective, and damaging to individuals and communities" (Isaacs and Lowen, 2007:p.39).

Solitary Watch reported in 2012 that "[t]he National Religious Campaign Against Torture..., citing negative budgetary, safety, and psychological effects of solitary confinement, argue that the 'excessive use of solitary confinement is a strain on our society and a moral and fiscal price we cannot afford to pay. Closing Tamms is not only common sense, it is a matter of conscience.'" (Rodriguez, 2012). Most poignantly though, the AFSC-Philadelphia, nearly a decade earlier, stated that the "larger community is... gravely harmed... by the profound erosion of our simple humanity. Here, as in every arena of life, violence only breeds more violence. Institutionalizing the use of violence can never solve the problems that violence created, in our communities or in our world" (Kamel and Kerness, 2003:p.12).

So, altogether, the United Nations, the AFSC, Human Rights Watch, Amnesty International, the John Howard Association, the MacArthur Justice Center, and many others who have reviewed our control units and supermax prisons have concluded that they basically amount to modern day torture chambers and are detrimental to the health of society. These organizations and a handful of others are bucking society's animosity towards prisoners to challenge the existence and necessity of these places and the prolonged isolation of people in them.

Encouragingly, it is not solely the liberal or progressive groups (which routinely fight for the rights of the oppressed) that are acknowledging that supermaxes, control units, and prolonged isolation in general are counterproductive. The courts, certain politicians, and even some correctional officials are also beginning to recognize this fact as well.

With the passage of both the Prison Litigation Reform Act (PLRA) and the Anti-Terrorism and Effective Death Penalty Act (AEDPA) in

1996, the nation's court systems have grown increasingly antagonistic towards anything filed by, or on behalf of, prisoners. Nevertheless, some judges are still willing to call a spade a spade when ruling on these facilities. According to John Maki of the JHA, "[t]hroughout the country, courts are discrediting the use of long-term isolation" (Maki, 2012b:p.3). Additionally, Dr. Stuart Grassian noted in an interview with Leo Grieb that:

> The courts have recognized that solitary confinement itself can cause a very specific kind of psychiatric syndrome, which in its worst stages can lead to an agitated, hallucinatory, confused psychotic state often involving random violence and self-mutilation, suicidal behavior, [and other] agitated, fearful and confusional kinds of symptoms (Kamel and Kerness, 2003:p.3).

For instance, in *Davenport v. DeRobertis*, Judge Richard Posner ruled in 1988 that, "the record shows, what anyway seems pretty obvious, that isolating a human being from other human beings year after year or even month after month can cause psychological damage...." and "there is plenty of medical and psychological literature concerning the ill effects of solitary confinement." In 1995, the court in *Madrid v. Gomez*, ruled that confining mentally ill people in supermaxes is "[t]he mental equivalent of putting an asthmatic in a place with little air to breathe," and "may press the outer bounds of what most humans can psychologically tolerate." In 1998, the court in *McClary v. Kelly* ruled that "[the fact that] prolonged isolation from social and environmental stimulation increases the risk of developing mental illness does not strike the Court as rocket science." In 2001, courts found that "[c]onfinement in supermaximum security prison...is known to cause psychiatric morbidity, disability, suffering and mortality" (*Jones 'El v. Burge*), and that solitary confinement units "are virtual incubators of psychosis-seeding illness in those already suffering from mental infirmities" (*Ruiz v. Johnson*).

Despite all of this, the U.S. Supreme Court has not banned the use of prolonged isolation by simply saying that it violates a person's Eighth Amendment Right to be free from cruel and unusual punishment. Therefore, tens of thousands of U.S. citizens continue to be confined in these units for years or even decades on end. Nor has the public risen up in most states to demand the closure of supermaxes. In most states, the public is either ignorant or indifferent to their existence, if not outright enamored by the correctional agencies' shiny new toys.

Some states and correctional agencies are beginning to see the folly of their ways though. As noted earlier, Colorado added 300 beds to its supermax system in 2010, but just two years later Jacob McCleland would report that "Colorado reduced its numbers from 1,500 to about 900 over the past year and will shut down a facility that's only two years old" (McCleland, 2012). Unfortunately, they didn't reduce the population fast enough, nor provide treatment to the inmates in isolation on a scale sufficient to prevent the psychotic break of Evan Ebel.

Mississippi took even more drastic measures. After experiencing "an increasing number of violent acts" they "decided to close their equivalent to a 'supermax', Unit 32" (Gustitus, 2012), rather than expand it like many other states do when confronted with the same circumstances. According to the *Rockford Register Star*, Mississippi "found that by bringing the prisoners into the general population and providing programming and human connection that violence was reduced and significant cost savings realized" (Ibid.).

"A similar result occurred in Maine" (Ibid.). In Maine, they adopted reforms to reduce their segregation unit from 130 inmates to around 40 and "[v]iolent incidents in the general population have also decreased" (McCleland, 2012). "Virginia has converted its supermax facility into a maximum security prison" (Felshman, 2008).

So, with adequate programming implemented, rather than seeing increased violence, the opposite occurs when these supposedly "worst of the worst" are released into the general population. This disproves the often-repeated claim that only supermaxes can control these prisoners and keep the prison staff and other inmates throughout the system safe. As John Maki noted, "the experience of prison systems in other states like Mississippi and Colorado have shown that the practice of long-term isolation is psychologically damaging and does not serve a legitimate correctional purpose" (Maki, 2012a).

Unfortunately, few states are willing to implement these proven programs and shutter their supermaxes. The AFSC quickly learned that the story of prisoner abuse in supermaxes "is not a story that the public seems to want to hear" (Magnani, 2003:p.1). Without the public outraged little will change. Without the public even learning of the conditions in, and facts about, these institutions, it is even less likely that a sufficient number of people will become outraged. Many politicians still support these places simply to maintain their tough-on-crime credentials. Guards' unions fight to keep them open to maintain the jobs they supply. Both politicians and guards' unions are usually quite knowledgeable about both the conditions and the facts surrounding supermaxes and the threats they pose, yet self-interest usually trumps common sense.

Surprisingly, the federal government is finally starting to examine the conditions in the country's supermaxes and control units. With an audience of over 250, congress held its first ever hearing on solitary confinement. Held in June of 2012 in front of the United States Senate Committee on the Judiciary Subcommittee on the Constitution, Civil Rights and Human Rights, it was titled "Reassessing Solitary Confinement: The Human Rights, Fiscal and Public Safety Consequences" (Friedmann, 2012:p.1). Vermont Senator Patrick Leahy explained that "[i]n the face of mounting evidence that the use of solitary confinement may in fact be counterproductive, this hearing is an excellent opportunity for the Committee to get a better understanding of this practice" (Ibid.).

They then heard testimony from former prisoners, psychiatrists, etc. U.S. Senator Dick Durbin from Illinois, who was instrumental in that hearing had toured Tamms a year or two earlier and pronounced everything hunky-dory to the press in the parking lot. After an intense backlash by anti-Tamms activists, and learning that the IDOC administration had hoodwinked him by concocting a facade of Tamms for his tour, Durbin quickly altered his stance and began having hearings.

Two years later though, they were still having hearings. Andrew Cohen would report in the *Atlantic* in February of 2014 that:

> On Capitol Hill Tuesday the Senate Judiciary Committee, Senator Richard Durbin (D-Ill.) presiding, will hold its second hearing in eight months on the topic of solitary confinement. Two simple facts about it tell you what you need to know about how far the issue has come in the past few years. First, the title of the proceedings is "Reassessing Solitary Confinement II: The Human Rights, Fiscal and Public Safety Consequences." Second, public interest in the hearing was so great that the venue for it had to be changed to a bigger room (Cohen, 2014).

It will be interesting to see if any changes in policy result from all of these hearings or not. Even when Illinois legislators learned of conditions at Tamms, they could never muster sufficient votes for reform.

Illinois is actually a perfect case study in the struggle to close a supermax prison - an incredibly expensive prison with no legitimate correctional purpose. Illinois followed the rest of the country in the rush to add a supermax prison to its prison system. In order to get legislation passed to fund construction and authorize its operation, the legislature was told that it would be used as a sort of short-term shock treatment to control the allegedly "worst of the worst" (*Associated Press*, 2012d; Lampert, 2009). As the *Chicago Reader* reported:

> The 1993 Illinois Task Force Report on Crime and Corrections specified that "the fundamental principle underlying the Supermax institution is that it is a management tool for addressing specific security problems that hinder delivery of essential services and anti-recidivism activities to the general population - it is *not* simply a place to put 500 inmates in an otherwise overcrowded system. To serve its purpose, inmates must move in *and out*, based on some objective classification and standards" (Felshman, 2008).

The legislation for Tamms easily passed through the legislature and construction was completed in 1997 at a cost of $70 million. Tamms Supermax Prison would open the next year with inmates being transferred to it without warning or explanation, and little hope to leave any time soon.

Within a few years of opening its steel, perforated cell doors to inmates, attorney Jean Maclean Snyder would inform the Illinois House Prison Management and Reform Committee in 2001 that: "[w]hen Tamms opened in March 1998, the word was that prisoners would have to serve a year there. After that, if they behaved they could be transferred out. But it's been three years now, and only a handful of prisoners have graduated from Tamms. Every month that passes with nobody moving out makes it harder to understand the rationale for this prison" (Snyder, 2001). The House Committee seemingly responded with a collective yawn as they failed to take any action to reform Tamms.

Concerned about the fate of their loved ones who were now trapped in these harsh conditions with no end in sight, the friends and families of Tamms prisoners began meeting and created the Tamms Committee.

In 2006, this spawned the Tamms Poetry Committee, which began mailings of poems to all Tamms prisoners to try and lift their spirits.

By this time "Tamms Supermax Prison" had undergone two name changes to try and be more media savvy and claim it wasn't a supermax. First, it was re-christened a "closed-maximum security prison" or "Tamms C-Max Prison" , then it was changed to "Tamms Correctional Center" in an attempt to make it indistinguishable from the similarly-named minimum security unit, which, although a completely separate facility, was located just a stone's throw away.

To this day though, the now empty supermax is located at 8500 Supermax Road. The town used to even have a sign that read "Welcome to Tamms, Home of the Supermax." At no time during its operation did the security classification descend. The only change was the name.

By 2008, the Tamms Poetry Committee would further spawn Tamms Year Ten, "a statewide campaign to persuade Illinois legislators and the governor to reform or close Tamms" (Tamms Year Ten,2012). Although there was a huge outcry at the time to close Guantanamo Bay, the public in general couldn't have cared less about all the little Gitmos in their own backyard, nor the Americans suffering inside them. Thus, Tamms Year Ten (TYT) had little doubt about the enormity of the task they were undertaking.

One of TYT's organizers, and its most ardent warrior, Laurie Jo Reynolds, "never thought she'd see [Tamms] closed" (*Associated Press*, 2012d). As reported by the *Chicagotribune.com*:

> "A lot of legislators, you just said the word 'Tamms' and they were like, 'Forget it. We want Tamms, we need Tamms. You're talking about murderers'", Reynolds said. "It was just a very difficult sell" (Ibid.).

She would similarly tell *In These Times* that, "[w]hen we first started this work, few people knew about the extent of this problem. Since then, we've seen growing public recognition that solitary confinement is a form or torture, and a real movement take hold" (Burns, 2013:p.11).

Tamms Year Ten was warned by veteran prison reformers "of the dangers of taking the issue of long-term solitary confinement directly to the public and press" (Tamms Year Ten, 2012). TYT chose to do just that regardless. They lobbied state legislators and then-Governor Pat Quinn, held coordinated prayer vigils across the state which received local news coverage at each site, and even picketed outside *The Chicago Tribune's* office when its editorial board ran an editorial supporting Tamms.

The same year TYT was formed, a study would conclude that, not only is Tamms not cost-effective, but it is "primarily a symbol, a gesture of overwhelming control," according to Jody L. Sundt, one of the study's co-authors (Pawlacyzyk and Hunsdorfer, 2009b). This would help TYT bring the message to fiscal conservatives.

TYT's most successful action in bringing their message to the public though, was their tactical media campaign in the summer of 2009. By teaming up with artists, TYT tagged up Chicago with six-feet by nine-feet mud stencils depicting a map of Illinois with a star locating Tamms and bold letters proclaiming "END TORTURE IN ILLINOIS" (Lampert, 2009). Jesse Graves, a Milwaukee artist, designed the stencils and thirty volunteers roamed the City plastering them on walls, sidewalks, and underpasses. They even tagged up tourist attractions like Navy Pier and the Chicago Zoo, as well as Logan Square Skate Park and numerous art institutes and museums (Ibid.).

This grassroots collaboration got many to take notice, most importantly the press. Numerous newspapers, magazines, and websites reported on it. Nicolas Lampert from Justseeds Radical Artists posted that the "action was designed to draw attention to the supermax in Illinois," because, as Laurie Jo Reynolds noted, "[m]any people don't realize that our supermax is more isolating than Guantanamo Bay, where identical treatment has been judged by Attorney General Eric Holder to be too isolating for prisoner safety" (Ibid.).

She said that "people were surprised to see the word torture being used in connection with the state of Illinois" (Ibid.). Such surprise shows how forgetful or clueless the public can be about what occurs in our criminal justice system. After all, this was at a time when former Chicago Police Lieutenant Jon Burge was still making headlines for torturing dozens of innocent people into falsely confessing and the city was repeatedly paying out seven- and eight-figure checks to compensate his victims.

"[W]hen [TYT] read [Tamms] inmates' testimony at public events, and described conditions at Tamms, [they] saw audiences react with horror and outrage" (Tamms Year Ten, 2012), and "[w]hen some progressive Illinois legislators were shown the facts, they too were ready to act" (Ibid.). These legislators helped craft legislation to try and force reform on Tamms. Although they were unsuccessful in getting it passed through the General Assembly, it did come close enough to scare the crap out of the IDOC administration and prompt then-Director Michael P. Randle to construct and begin implementing a "10-Point-Plan" to bring some much-needed reforms, like G.E.D. testing and telephone calls, to Tamms in 2011.

By 2009, even Cook County Sheriff Tom Dart would admit that long-term solitary confinement "doesn't really work" (Pawlacyzyk and Hundsdorfer, 2009b) . Nevertheless, it was still nearly impossible for an inmate to win a transfer out of Tamms unless they were completing their prison sentence or had "successfully renounced" and provided information to the administration about the activities of other inmates. It would be reported that year that "one-third of prisoners [at Tamms] have been held indefinitely since the prison opened over ten years ago" (Lampert, 2009).

In 2010, things began to change with a federal district court ruling in July. The case, *Westefer v. Snyder*, would be a game-changer for Tamms. The court ruled that, not only did the conditions at Tamms constitute an "atypical and significant hardship" compared to ordinary prison life and compared to any other disciplinary segregation or administrative detention environment in the state, but since the conditions were so hard, inmates had a liberty interest in not being transferred to Tamms. Therefore, inmates had due process rights and the state had to provide notice and justification for the transfer to Tamms as well as a hearing where inmates could defend themselves (*Westefer v. Snyder*, 2010).

Nearly everyone at Tamms had to be given a hearing as a result, and dozens of inmates would win transfers in the following two years, as they challenged the adequacy of both the hearings themselves and the previously undisclosed (and often fabricated) rationale for their transfer to Tamms. The administration struggled to replace the transferred inmates (as now they had to justify each transfer to Tamms) and the population started to decrease for the first time since Tamms opened. Within two years though, *Westefer v. Snyder* would be overturned. The federal appellate court would find that the district court had violated the PLRA and had overstepped its bounds by requiring the IDOC to provide notice, justification, and a hearing to inmates.

The year 2012 turned out to be a whirlwind of activity and a constant back and forth battle for public opinion, with the American Federation of State County and Municipal Employees (AFSCME), (the prison guard's union) on one side, and then-Governor Pat Quinn, Tamms Year Ten, and other anti-Tamms activists on the other.

In February, Quinn took everyone by surprise when he announced his intention to close Tamms for good. With Illinois in a fiscal mess and a $43.8 billion budget deficit, Quinn claimed his decision was strictly a belt-tightening measure. He noted that it cost three times as much to incarcerate someone at Tamms than other adult prisons in the state, and was only half full (Ruthhart, 2012;p.5.). Closing Tamms would save the state its annual $26 million operating budget (Burns, 2013:p.10).

Although Quinn claimed it was all about money to the press, *The News-Gazette* would later report that "[Quinn has] been convinced by inmate advocates that being held at Tamms is simply too cruel a punishment to inflict on any inmate, no matter how badly the inmate has behaved in prison" (*The News-Gazette*, 2012).

AFSCME immediately and vociferously voiced its opposition to closing Tamms. They first claimed that it would "endanger guards and inmates alike" (O'Connor, 2012), but this assertion became just a rote accusation. TYT would accuse AFSCME of fear-mongering as a result (Burns, 2013:p.10). If AFSCME truly feared increased violence they would have pushed for increased programming which had worked so well to reduce violence in other prison systems. Instead, they chose to keep fighting to keep Tamms open, even though studies had already shown that isolation only works to make both inmates and staff alike more angry and violent. As time went on, the public started to realize what the true cause of concern for the union was, one that AFSCME began promoting as their primary justification for opposing the closure of Tamms, and the only argument that actually had some logic (however twisted) behind it. It was that closure of Tamms would mean the loss of about 300 union jobs (Keyser, 2012b; *Associated Press*, 2012b).

On April 2nd, the Midwest Coalition for Human Rights, the ACLU Stop Solitary Campaign, and Tamms Year Ten brought witnesses from around the country to a hearing on Tamms in Ulin, Illinois (Tamms Year Ten, 2012). Two day later TYT took the fight to AFSCME. "[O]n the 44th anniversary of [Martin Luther King, Jr's] death, [they] held the I AM A MOM March" (Ibid.). This was a tactic meant to shame AFSCME for its opposition to closing Tamms. TYT "wanted to both celebrate AFSCME's progressive past and put the union on the spot for their hypocrisy in fighting to keep Tamms open" (Ibid.). They held signs that read "I AM A MOM" - "an allusion to AFSCME's famous 1968 'I AM A MAN' campaign for striking sanitation workers in Memphis" (Burns, 2013:p.10), where AFSCME marched beside MLK, Jr. (Ibid.). Other signs held by TYT protesters read things like "MY SON IS NOT A PAYCHECK", "MY BROTHER *IS* A HUMAN BEING", and "WE SUPPORT UNIONS THAT SUPPORT HUMAN RIGHTS".

According to *MSN News Center*, "[t]he demonstrators marched to the union's headquarters on Chicago's Michigan Avenue, shouting, 'No more torture. No more cages'. They said they sympathized with the southern community's economic plight but the issue was about human rights and dignity, not jobs. 'A job in which you are essentially torturing people is not a job worth keeping', said Stephen Eisenman, one of the organizers and a professor at Northwestern University" (Keyser, 2012a).

Three weeks later TYT "held a thank you vigil for [torture survivor and] U.N. Special Rapporteur on Torture Juan E. Mendez when he spoke at the University of Chicago in May. Mothers and other family members held up long-stemmed white roses and signs to thank him for his report [in 2011] officially calling for a ban on solitary confinement in excess of 15 days. [TYT] submitted an official report requesting that the United Nations investigate claims of torture at Tamms....[Mendez] was treating these complaints under special procedures through a confidential exchange of notes between the government of the United States and the United Nations" (Tamms Year Ten, 2012).

On May 1st, Illinois' Commission on Government Forecasting and Accountability "recommended against Gov. Pat Quinn's plan to close" Tamms (Groeninger, 2012). AFSCME quickly praised the recommendation (Ibid.).

On June 29th, Quinn offered to sell Tamms to the federal government (*Associated Press*, 2012b). This would be the second prison Illinois unloads on the feds in recent years if the sale goes through (Thompson Correctional Center was sold to the Feds in 2012).

June 29th was also the day that the governor received "budget legislation which include[d] money to keep Tamms open" (Ibid.). In order to secure that funding, an agreement was struck among legislators that would have repurposed Tamms as a medium-security prison. The governor was not a party to that deal though, and, intent on closing Tamms, he promptly blocked the funding (Keyser, 2012b).

The John Howard Association would note that "[r]epurposing Tamms for other correctional ends is impractical because it would entail modifications that are cost-prohibitive, particularly in light of the fact that DOC has been asked to cut more than $100 million from its fiscal year 2013 budget, an almost 10 percent reduction from 2012" (Szilak, 2012:p.5).

Quinn's plan was for Tamms to be shuttered by August 31st. On August 2nd, the "first eight Tamms inmates were transferred out" (O'Connor, 2012). Six hours later, AFSCME filed suit in Alexander County, where Tamms is located, seeking to halt the closure of Tamms and an injunction against further transfers until the suit concluded (Ibid.; Garcia, 2012). The judge granted the injunction putting a halt to transfers out of Tamms (Burns, 2012:p.10).

The parties were then sent before a state labor arbitrator (Ibid.). Additionally, Quinn had appealed the granting of the injunction to the state appellate court. It was both good news and bad news for the governor and Tamms inmates in October. While the arbitrator ruled in Quinn's favor, the appellate court refused to lift the injunction. (Ibid.).

In the meantime, TYT remained active, advocating and lobbying for closure. Numerous public events were held, but "[a]s time passed, it got harder to engage the press about the merits of closing Tamms" (Tamms Year Ten, 2012), so they started pitching other Tamms-related stories to show the humanity of Tamms inmates. They got both *The Chicago Tribune* and *Chicago Public Radio* to run stories about a TYT project where inmates could request photos to be taken and sent to them (Ibid.).

In November, state legislators who opposed closing Tamms and some other facilities made a final effort to override the governor's veto of funding for those facilities. On November 28th "the Senate passed by a landslide a motion to override Quinn's veto," but "a week later the House refused to take up the override measure"(Ibid.). According to TYT:

> This was due to a combination of factors: a *Chicago Tribune* editorial chiding individual Senators for their vote to fund empty prisons; a damning article about Tamms in the *Belleville News Democrat*; and Republican leader Tom Cross's public statement that he would vote to sustain Governor Quinn's veto. It was also because of our intense phone call and lobbying campaign. Many advocates banded together to help us (Ibid.).

This failure to override the governor's veto sounded the death knell for Tamms. Less than two weeks later, the Illinois Supreme Court would order Alexander County Circuit Court Judge Charles Cabaness to dissolve the injunction, which he did a week later (Ibid.).

That day, December 19th, 2012, twenty-five more men were transferred out of Tamms (Ibid.). By the 28th there would be no inmates left in Tamms, a prison less than 15 years old (*Associated Press* 2012c and 2012d). The prison would be shuttered by January 4th, 2013 when the last employees would likewise leave Tamms (Ibid.).

In a letter to supporters, TYT noted how:

> In the beginning, Quinn's office only emphasized the empty and half-empty prisons. By the end, the governor's office noted that Tamms was condemned by human rights monitors for violating international standards for the humane treatment of prisoners, and even quoted MLK, Jr. "It is always the right time to do the right thing"(Tamms Year Ten, 2012).

So, although the fight to change public opinion and get a supermax closed may seem like an insurmountable task, the case of Illinois shows that it can be done.

In 2012, the Heartland Alliance's National Immigrant Justice Center and Physicians for Human Rights issued a damning report on the use of isolation for "illegal" immigrants in the custody of U.S. Immigration and Customs Enforcement (ICE)(*Prison Legal News*, 2014:p.44). ICE was placing detainees in solitary confinement "simply because they were mentally ill, due to their sexual orientation or because they could not speak English" (Ibid.). Surprisingly, the report has prompted a policy change by ICE (Ibid.). The new policy states, "[p]lacement in segregation should occur only when necessary and in compliance with applicable detention standards and that "placement in administrative segregation due to a special vulnerability should be used only as a last resort and when no other viable housing options exist" (Ibid:p.45). Time will tell whether the policy change will result in an actual change in practice, but it's a start.

Even some guards are beginning to switch sides. *The Atlantic* reported that in January of 2014 "the largest prison guard union in Texas called for the curtailment of the use of solitary on the state's death row. Let me say that again; Prison guards in Texas...have come to believe that isolating prisoners in this fashion is self-defeating" (Cohen, 2014).

The article's author noted:

> Something clearly is happening here and it's not just based upon some slight uptick in public acknowledgment of the immorality of confining fellow human beings to such cruelty no matter what their crimes. There is movement here because there is growing evidence that inhumane treatment of prisoners is neither safe nor efficient.

> There is movement here because there is now a strong economic case for prison reform. There is movement, in other words, even though there still is an overwhelming lack of empathy toward the punished (Cohen, 2014).

The good news is that momentum is gaining to cease using long-term isolation. In 2014," the state of New York agreed to ban the use of extreme isolation for juveniles and limit its use with adults" (Clarke and Maki, 2014). Durbin and other U.S. Senators are calling for a complete nationwide ban on isolating juveniles (Ibid.). The Federal Bureau of Prisons claimed to have reduced solitary confinement by 25% between 2013 and 2014 (Ibid.). Most surprising of all, in 2015 even President Obama, using the biggest bully pulpit in the world, began to call for decreasing the use of solitary confinement, and this year ordered a ban on placing juveniles in long-term solitary confinement in federal facilities.

-STILL MUCH FURTHER TO GO-

The bad news is that we still have a long way to go to see the end of supermaxes and control units. Moreover, even when there is a victory, as was the case with the closing of Tamms, it is short-lived. Laurie Jo Reynolds, from Tamms Year Ten, has once again had to email supermax opponents to urge them to contact their legislators. This time, it is to try to prevent Tamms from being reopened.

During the last state election in Illinois, Pat Quinn lost the governorship to Republican Bruce Rauner, who had voiced support for reopening Tamms. The Republicans, overall, gained many seats in the Illinois General Assembly as well, and support for reopening Tamms among the party is strong. Luckily fiscal conservatives oppose such a waste of taxpayer funds during the current fiscal crisis Illinois finds itself in with the pension debt.(The Republicans have even filed legislation to try to reinstate the death penalty nevertheless.).

Even if Tamms doesn't reopen, the situation in Illinois is far from good. At most, Tamms held just shy of 300 men at one time. With the closure of Tamms, control units popped up at prisons across the state.

For a while, X-House in Stateville Correctional Center was a control unit, before it was mysteriously emptied less than a year later. There are still *hundreds* of men in the new control unit in Pontiac Correctional Center. The North House of Pontiac (where the other death row, and then the Tamms step-down were located) received nearly 100 Tamms transferees when Tamms closed in 2012. Thereafter, it expanded to consume the entire evens side of the four-story building. By 2013, the John Howard Association would report that, "on the day of JHA's visit [February 17, 2013], Pontiac housed more than 800 inmates in either administrative detention or long-term [over 2 years] disciplinary segregation" (Troyer, 2013:p.2).

In June of 2015, three inmates at Pontiac - Douglas Coleman, Aaron Fillmore and Jerome Jones - filed a "Class Action Complaint For Declatory And Injunctive Relief" (on behalf of all similarly situated inmates, in the United States District Court for the Northern District of Illinois (Eastern Division)) challenging "the State of Illinois' policies and customs, which place every individual incarcerated in Illinois at risk of being subjected to extraordinarily long and severely harmful extreme segregation sentences"(p.3). The complaint notes that "as of June 30, 2013, approximately 2,300 [IDOC inmates] were serving extreme isolation sentences" (p. 2).

There are also numerous other control units (or administrative detention units in IDOC parlance) that each hold dozens of men. They are often difficult to locate as the IDOC tries to keep their existence from becoming public knowledge. Little is known about the one at Lawrence Correctional Center. Much is known about the one at Menard Correctional Center where the inmates there have risked life and limb to get the word out. Inmates there have gone on hunger strikes and written to numerous newspapers around the country to try and expose the horrendous treatment of themselves and others isolated there. The conditions have even been recounted for the United States Senate. On February 25, 2014 attorney Alan Mills of Uptown People's Law Center submitted a "Statement For Senate Judiciary Subcommittee Hearing Reassessing Solitary Confinement II," describing the draconian conditions, how inmates are trapped in Menard's High Security Unit, and the arbitrary, Kafkaesque system that denies inmates there any legitimate due process to challenge their initial placement and/or their continued placement in Administrative Detention.

Many of the men at Pontiac, Lawrence, and Menard are ex-Tamms inmates. They have either never been allowed to return to general population, or once in general population, are, more often than not, accused of trumped-up charges as a pretext to send them back to isolation - either to disciplinary segregation or administrative detention in one of the various control units Illinois now maintains.

If you ask the IDOC how many people they have in administrative detention in the entire IDOC, as this author did in April of 2014, you'll get a one sentence answer without any supporting documentation. The figure they gave, "158 inmates" (Berg, 2014), is incredibly difficult to believe. Even if it were true, that would be 158 too many.

Furthermore, even though the Illinois Department of Corrections closed its stand-alone supermax facility, Illinois will now house another new supermax within its borders. After selling the Thompson Correctional Center to the federal government, Illinois learned that the Bureau of Prisons (which had long claimed they were reducing their use of solitary confinement) decided to turn the main facility into a supermax.

In April of 2014, Lisa Dawson of *Solitary Watch* would report the following:

> Even as it touts new initiatives to reduce the number of people it holds in solitary confinement, the federal Bureau of Prisons (BOP) continues to quietly make headway on the activation of Thompson Correctional Center in northwestern Illinois. If all proceeds as planned, Thompson will substantially increase the federal government's capacity to hold individuals in extreme isolation - a fact that no one, these days, seems to want to talk about.... Dubbed early on "Gitmo North," the facility was originally viewed by the Obama Administration as a possible future home for scores of terrorism suspects held by the U.S. at Guantanamo Bay military detention camp in Cuba... Thompson is slated to be an "Administrative Maximum U.S. Penitentiary"(ADX/USP)....The joint classification of Thompson as ADX/USP means that a portion of the new prison will also have a Maximum Security classification, which will include an SMU, or Special

Management Unit, where individuals are also held in 24 -hour lock-down, often with two or three people to a cell.... Backing the opening of ADX/USP is the same Sen. Dick Durbin (D-IL) who has built a reputation challenging the use of solitary confinement in U.S. prisons.... When asked by *Solitary Watch* about Durbin's support of a new federal supermax, spokesperson Max Gleisschman did not deny that Thompson would include ADX cells. He did not comment on the apparent contradiction in Durbin's position, except to say that no one would be "housed in segregation unnecessarily" (Dawson, 2014).

As we've seen though, one's definition of "necessary" can quickly become meaningless. The administrations of various prisons have long felt that it was "necessary" to isolate jailhouse lawyers, women who were victims of sexual assault by guards thereby making them more vulnerable, and just about anyone who was mentally ill. Hell, ICE felt it "necessary" to isolate anyone who was gay, transgender, or simply couldn't speak English. Like I said, we still have *much* further to go.

-CONCLUSION-

As Linda J. Gustitus wrote as a guest columnist for the *Rockford Register Star*, "[i]n short, the explosion of 'supermax' prisons was a costly mistake"(Gustitus, 2012). Not just in monetary terms either. Rather the cumulative effect they are having on the people confined in them, on the guards that work there, on the overall health of our society, and on the stated goals of our state and federal governments (i.e. to rehabilitate offenders, reduce crime, and use our limited resources wisely and for the betterment of society) has become an unnecessary threat to our national security.

The famous writer Ralph Ellison, speaking on *racial* segregation in his "Twentieth-Century Fiction and the Black Mask of Humanity" wrote the following about segregation:

> Perhaps the most insidious and least understood form of segregation is that of the word. And by this I mean the word in all its complex formulations, from the proverb to the novel and stage play, the word with all its subtle power to suggest and foreshadow overt action while magically disguising the moral consequences of that action and psychological justification. For if the word has the potency to revive and make us free, it has also the power to blind, imprison and destroy.

That statement is equally true of long-term segregation in prisons and jails. It is the height of folly for prison administrators, and society in general, to believe that they can ignore the immorality of their actions and treat people inhumanely and that there will be no repercussions. To do so not only poses a serious physical threat to society, but also erodes our moral fiber and stains the proclaimed moral integrity of our country (as we've seen with Abu Ghraib and Guantanamo Bay).

We are finally seeing the beginning of real resistance to the use of long term isolation, and one hopes a beginning to the end of the supermax era. Unfortunately, this is just the beginning. While we've seen a halt to the expansion of supermaxes, and a few have closed, it will take many more courageous and conscientious people to stand up to the status quo, inform the citizenry of the ill-effects these isolation chambers have on our society, and demand that the rest be dismantled.

-WORKS CITED-

The American Heritage Dictionary (2001). Fourth Edition. Bantam Dell Publishing (2001).

Associated Press (2012). "Mentally ill inmates sue to get out of solitary." *Foxnews.com*. May 17, 2012. *http://www.foxnews.com/ us/2012/05/17/mentally-ill-inmates-sue-to-get-out-solitary/print*.

Associated Press (2012b). "Quinn asks feds to buy Tamms prison." *Daily Herald*. Saturday, June 30, 2012: Section 1, p.6.

Associated Press (2012c). "Inmate transfers from Illinois prisons almost complete." December 24, 2012. *Chicagotribune.com*. www.chicagotribune.com/news/local/breaking/chi-inmate-transfers-from-illinois-prisons-almost-complete-20121224,0,1904071.story.

Associated Press (2012d). "Last inmates leave Tamms 'supermax' prison." December 28, 2012. *Chicago tribune.com*.

Berg, Ronald (2014). Illinois Department of Corrections email to IDOC FOIA Officer Lisa Weitekamp in response to FOIA Request made by author. Email sent April 16, 2014, 9:15 a.m.

Burnett, Sara (2011). "Supermax inmate suing to lessen solitary confinement." *The Denver Post*. April 29, 2011.

Burns, Rebecca (2013). "Supermax Showdown." *In These Times*. January 2013: p.10-11.

Clarke, Elizabeth, and Maki, John (2014). "End Solitary Confinement For Juveniles." *Chicago Sun-Times.com*. March 5, 2014, Updated March 6, 2014, 12:03a.m.

Coalition For Prisoners' Rights (2010a). "Solitary Watch Project." *Coalition For Prisoners' Rights Newsletter*. February 2010: Vol.35-b, No.2.

Coalition For Prisoners' Rights (2010b). "Solitary Confinement Changes." *Coalition For Prisoners' Rights Newsletter*. July 2010:Vol. 35-b, No.7.

Cohen, Andrew (2014). "American Exceptionalism, Crime-and-Punishment Edition." *Atlantic Monthly*. February 24, 2014.

Cusac, Ann-Marie (2000). "The Devil's Chair." *The Progressive*. April 2000.

Dannenberg, John (2014). "Systemic Changes Follow Murder Of Colorado Prison Director." *Prison Legal News*. Vol. 25, No. 7, July 2014: p.1-7.

Davenport v. DeRobertis, 844 F. 2d 1310, 1313 and 1316 (7th Cir.1988).

Dawson, Lisa (2014). "Funding Approved for Activation of ADX/USP Thompson, New Federal Supermax Prison." Report, *Solitary Watch*. Thursday, April 17, 2014.

Dowker, Fay, and Good, Glenn (1993). "The Proliferation of Control Unit Prisons in the United States." *Journal of Prisoners on Prisons*. Vol. 4, No. 2, 1993: p.107.

Eberhardt, Sally, and Theoharis, Jeanne (2011). "Stateside Gitmos." *The Nation*. February 7, 2011: p.9.

Eisenman, Stephen F., and Reynolds, Laurie Jo (2009). "Guantanamo Bay In Illinois? Downstate Supermax Holds 250 in Long-Term Isolation." *Capital City Courier*. February 2009.

Faris, R. E. (1962). "Cultural Isolation and the Schizophrenic Personality." *American Journal of Sociology*. September, 40 (2): 155-164.

Fellner, Jaime and Mariner, Joanne (1997). "Cold Storage: Super-Maximum Security Confinement in Indiana." Human Rights Watch. October 1997.

Felshman, Jeffrey (2008). "Hell in a Cell." *Chicago Reader*. April 24, 2008. *http://www.chicagoreader.com*.

Frey, Warden Shelton (2005). "Warden's Bulletin No. 05-06." Tamms Correctional Center. Illinois Department of Corrections. January 12, 2005.

Friedmann, Alex (2012). "Solitary Confinement Subject of Unprecedented Congressional Hearing." *Prison Legal News*. October 2012: Vol. 23, No. 10: p. 1-15.

Garcia, Monique (2012). "Union sues Quinn over planned prison closings." *The Chicago Tribune*. Friday, August 3, 2012: Section 1, p. 11.

Gibbons, John J., and de B. Katzenbach, Nicholas (2006). "Confronting Confinement: A Report Of The Commission On Safety And Abuse In America's Prisons." Vera Institute of Justice. June 2006. *www.prisoncommission.org*.

Grassian, Stuart, M. D. (1983). "Psychopathological Effects of Solitary Confinement." *American Journal of Psychiatry*, 140 (1983): p. 1450-1454.

Grassian, S., and Friedman, N. (1986). "Effects of Sensory Deprivation In Psychiatric Seclusion And Solitary Confinement." *International Journal of Law & Psychiatry*, 8: 49-65.

Groeninger, Alissa (2012). "State legislators oppose plan to close facilities." *The Chicago Tribune*. Wednesday, May 2, 2012: Section 1, p.9.

Gustitus, Linda J. (2012). Guest Column: Tamms 'supermax' prison in Illinois was a mistake." *rrstar.com* (*Rockford Register Star*) July 10, 2012.

Haney, C. (2003a). "Infamous punishment: the psychological consequences of isolation." *National Prison Project Journal*. 2003 (Spring):2- 21.

Haney, C. (2003b). Mental health issues in long-term solitary and "supermax" confinement. *Crime Delinqu*. 2003; 49 (1): 124-156.

Haney, Craig, and Lynch, Mona (1997). "Regulating Prisons of the Future: A Psychological Analysis of Supermax and Solitary Confinement." *New York University Review of Law and Social Change*. 23 (1997): 477-570.

Harper's Magazine (2012a). "Harper's Index." September 2012: p.13, citing the American Civil Liberties Union (Washington).

Harper's Magazine (2012b). "Harper's Index." September 2012: p.13, citing Craig Haney, University of California, Santa Cruz.

Human Rights Watch (2000). "Out of Sight. HRW Briefing Paper on Supermaximum Prisons." Human Rights Watch. 2000. http://www.hrw.org/reports/2000/supermax/Sprmx002.htm.

In re Medley, 134 U.S. 160, 10 S.Ct. 384, 33 L.Ed. 835 (March 3,1890). United State Supreme Court.

Isaacs, Caroline, and Lowen, Matthew (2007). "Buried Alive: Solitary Confinement in Arizona's Prisons and Jails." American Friends Service Committee-Arizona. May 2007.

Istanbul Statement on the Use and Effects of Solitary Confinement (2007). Adopted on 9 December 2007 at the International Psychological Trauma Symposium, Istanbul. *Torture*. Volume 18, Number 1:

p. 63-66 (2008).

Johnson, Kevin (2005). "After Years in Solitary, Freedom Hard to Grasp." *USA Today*. June 9, 2005.

Jones' El v. Burge, 164 F. Supp. 1096, at 1118 (2001).

Kamel, Rachel, and Kerness, Bonnie (2003). "The Prison Inside the Prison: Control Units, Supermax Prisons, and Devices of Torture." American Friends Service Committee-Philadelphia, 2003.

Kerness, Bonnie (2009). "Control Units: Illegal Torture Not Just for Guantanamo." *WIN Magazine*. Fall 2009.

Keyser, Jason (2012a). "Moms support closure of Illinois supermax prison." *MSN News Center*. April 5, 2012.

Keyser, Jason (2012b). "Quinn blocks prison funds." *Daily Herald*. Sunday, July 1, 2012: Section 1, p. 15.

Korn, R. (1998). "The Effects of Confinement in the High Security Unit at Lexington." *Social Justice*. 15(1): 8-19.

Kozar, Richard (2001). *John McCain (Overcoming Adversity)*. Chelsea House Publishing, 2001.

Kukorowski, Drew (2012). "The Price to Call Home: State-Sanctioned Monopolization in the Prison Phone Industry." *Prison Legal News*. October, 2012. Vol. 23, No. 10: p. 20-24.

Kupers, Terry A., and Moltz, David (2010). "Solitary confinement poses a danger to everyone." *Bangor Daily News*. Posted February 25, 2010 at 6:57 p.m.

Kurki, Lenna, and Morris, Norval (2001). "The purposes, practices and problems of supermax prisons." IN: Tonry M. ed. *Crime and Justice:A Review of Research*. Chicago, Ill.: University of Chicago Press, 2001:385-424.

Lampert, Nicolas (2009). "Illinois Torture Publicized with Ecological Art: Chicago and Milwaukee Artists Boost Tamms Year Ten Message With Mud Stencils." *www.justseeds.org*. June 7, 2009.

Larson, Doran (2014). "American Apartheid: Why Scandinavian Prisons Are Superior." *Prison Legal News*. Vol. 25, No. 1, January 2014: p.3.

Law, Victoria (2014). "Women In Solitary Confinement: 'The Isolation Degenerates Us Into Madness.'" *Prison Legal News*. October

2014: p.12- 15 (originally published in two parts by *Solitary Watch* in December 2013. *www.solitarywatch.com.*).

Lelyveld, Joseph (2011). "What 9/11 Wrought." *Smithsonian.* September, 2011: p.62-63.

Liebelson, Dana (2015). "They Locked Me In That Little Room With Nothing." *Mother Jones.* January/February 2015: p.48-53.

Lovell, D., Cloyes, C., Allen, D. G., and Rhodes, L.A. (2000). "Who lives in supermaximum custody?" A Washington State study. *Fed. Probat.* 2000: 61: 3: 40-45.

Madrid v. Gomez, 889 F. Supp. 1146, at 1265 (N.D. Cal. 1995).

Magnani, Laura (2008). "Buried Alive: Long-Term Isolation in California's Youth and Adult Prisons." American Friends Service Committee-Oakland, May 2008.

Maki, John (2012a). "JHA Supports Governor Quinn's Proposed Closure of Tamms." John Maki, Executive Director. John Howard Association, 2012.

Maki, John (2012b). *Stateville Speaks Newsletter.* Summer, 2012: p.3.

Mandela, Nelson (1993). *The Long Walk to Freedom.* 1995.

Manor, Robert (2010a). "Monitoring Tour of Menard Correctional Center." John Howard Association. April 6, 2010.

Manor, Robert (2010b). "Monitoring Tour of Tamms Supermax Prison." John Howard Association. November 9, 2010.

Manor, Robert, and Maki, John (2010). "Cuts in Prison Education Put Illinois at Risk." John Howard Association. Executive Summary.

Matthews, Cara (2006). "Mentally Ill Inmates' Treatment Decried." *The Democrat and Chronicle.* (Rochester, NY). June 8, 2006. http://democratandchronicle.com/apps/pbcs/dll/frontpage.

McClary v. Kelly, 4 F. Supp. 2d 195, at 208 (1098).

McCleery, R. (1961). Authoritarianism and the Belief System of the Incorrigibles. IN: Cressey, D. (ed.) *The Prison.* New York: Holt Rhinehart and Winston, pp. 260-306.

McCleland, Jacob (2012). "The High Costs Of High Security At Supermax Prisons." *www.npr.org.* June 19, 2012. Last accessed June 25, 2012.

Mosso, G.E.(1997). "The Truth About Prison Education." *Prison Connections*. Winter,1997,Volume 1,Number 3.

Motel, Mel (2012). "PLN Readers Flood FCC with Letters: Campaign Fights for Prison Phone Justice." *Prison Legal News,* November,2012:p.20-21.

The News-Gazette(2012). "Slamming Door on Tamms." Monday, December 31,2012. http://www.news-gazette.com .

New York Times (2014). The Editorial Board. "End Mass Incarceration Now." May 24,2014.

O'Connor, John(2012). "AP News Break: Tamms inmates moved on day of lawsuit." Thursday, August 2, 2012. *http://www.sfgate.com*.

O'Connor, John(2015). "Ex-Tamms inmate accused in prison stabbing." *Associated Press*. Tuesday, March 24, 2015.

Ortiz, Vikki (2008). "'Supermax' prison reforms urged: Lawmakers, ex-inmates gather to announce bill." *The Chicago Tribune*. Monday, May 26, 2008.

O'Shea, Patrick(1993). "A Tour Through The Circles of Hell." *Odyssey*. Spring,1993:p.34-43.

Pawlacyzyk, George, and Hundsdorfer, Beth(2009a). "Trapped in Tamms: Illinois' only supermax facility, inmates are in cells 23 hours a day." *Prisonmovement'sWeblog*. August 2, 2009. http://prisonmovement.worpress.com

Pawlacyzyk, George, and Hundsdorfer, Beth(2009b). "Is it worth it? State spends $92,000 per inmate per year to run Tamms prison."*Belleville News-Democrat*. Thursday, December 31,2009. *http://www.belleville.com*.

Prendergast, Alan(2012). "Troy Anderson Lawsuit: Supermax conditions draw criticism from judge." Monday, May 7, 2012.

Prison Legal News(2014). "ICE Implements New Directive to Limit Solitary Confinement."October, 2014:Vol.25,No.l0,p.44-45.

Reardon, Sara(2012), "INSIGHT: Maths joins the war on drug cartels."*New Scientist*. 20 October 2012:p.l2.

Reyes, H. (2007). "The worst scars are in the mind: psychological torture." *International Review of the Red Cross*. Vol.89,No.867.September,2007: p.591-617.

Rhodes, Lorne A., PhD.(2005). "Pathological Effects of the Supermaximum Prison."*American Journal of Public Health*. October 2005,Vol.95,No.10: p. 1692-1695.

Ridgeway, James, and Casella, Jean(2010). "Maine Legislature Votes to Study Solitary Confinement Practices - But Not to Change Them." *Solitary Watch*. April 7,2010.

Ridgeway, James, and Casella, Jean(2011). "Cruel and Unusual Solitary Confinement in U.S. Prisons."*Solitary Watch Newsletter*. Spring 2011.

Ridgeway, James, and Casella, Jean(2012). "Leading Mental Health Experts Urge Illinois Legislators to Close Tamms Supermax."*Solitary Watch*. March 29,2012(Reprinting "Comments by Dr. Stuart Grassian, Dr. Craig Haney, and Dr. Terry Kupers to the April 2,2012 Hearing of the Illinois Legislature Commission on Government Forecasting and Accountability regarding the proposal to close Tamms Correctional Center.").

Rodriguez, Sal(2012). "Testimony from Hearing on Closure of Tamms Supermax Prison." *Solitary Watch*. April 21, 2012.

Ruiz v. Johnson,154 F.Supp.2d 975(S.D.Tex.2001).

Ruthhart, Bill(2012). "Quinn's budget swap: Governor set to veto spending on prisons he plans to shut in bid to restore $50 million for DCFS." *The Chicago Tribune*. Saturday , June 30 , 2012 : Section 1,p.l and 5.

Scott, G.D., and Gendreau, P. (1969). "Psychiatric Implications of Sensory Deprivation in a Maximum Security Prison." *Canadian Psychiatric Association Journal*. 14 (1): 337-341.

Shalev, Sharon (2008). "A Sourcebook on Solitary Confinement." Mannheim Centre for Criminology (London, UK).

Snyder, Jean Maclean (2001). "Statement to the Illinois House Prison Management and Reform Legislation Committee." Thompson Center, Chicago, IL. April 27, 2001.

Solitary Watch Newsletter (2011). "Confronting Torture in U.S. Prisons: A Q & A with Solitary Watch." Summer 2011: p. 3.

Stromberg, Joseph (2014). "The Science of Solitary Confinement: Research tells us that isolation is an ineffective rehabilitation strategy and leaves lasting psychological damage." *smithsonianmag.com*. February 19, 2014.

Subways, Suzy (2011). "Fasting For Human Rights in Secure Housing Units of California." *Prison Health News*. Issue 11. Summer 2011: p. 5 (Philadelphia, PA).

Szilak, Maya (2012). "A Price Illinois Cannot Afford: Tamms and the Costs of Long-Term Isolation." The John Howard Association, 2012. *www. thejha.org.*

Tamms Year Ten (2012). Letter to friends in Tamms and friends who have once been in Tamms. December 20, 2012.

Tapley, Lance (2012). "Solitary Confinement: Bad for Chimps, Okay for Humans." *Prison Legal News*. October 2012: Vol. 23, No. 10: p.16.

Tietz, Jeff (2012). "Slow-Motion Torture: How solitary confinement - once reserved for the most dangerous and disobedient inmates - became standard practice in American Prisons." *Rolling Stone*. December 6, 2012: p. 58-66.

Toch, H. (1999). IN: Kupers, T. *Prison Madness: The Mental Health Crisis Behind Bars and What We Must Do About It*. San Francisco, California : Jossey-Bass Publishers; 1999: ix-xiv.

Troyer, Gwyneth, et al. (2013). *Monitoring Visit to Pontiac Correctional Center 2013*. John Howard Association. Chicago, IL. n.d.

Troyer, Gwyneth, and Maki, John, et al. (2014). *2013 Update Monitoring Visit to Menard Correctional Center*. John Howard Association. Chicago , IL. n.d.

Wakefield, D. (1980). "A Thousand Days of Solitary." National Prisoner's Movement. London, UK.

Welborn, Warden George C. (1999). "Warden's Bulletin No. 99-88." Tamms Correctional Center. Illinois Department of Corrections. June 30, 1999.

Westefer v. Snyder, Case No. 3:00-cv-00162-GPM (7/20/10) (Document 540) United States District Court for the Southern District of Illinois.

Wilson, N.K. (1991). "Hard-Core Prisoners Controlled in Nation's High- Tech Prisons." *Chicago Daily Law Bulletin*. April 25, 1991: p.2.

The World Almanac And Book Of Facts: 2012. World Almanac Books (New York, NY). November 2011.

-ABOUT THE AUTHOR-

-JOSEPH RODNEY DOLE II-

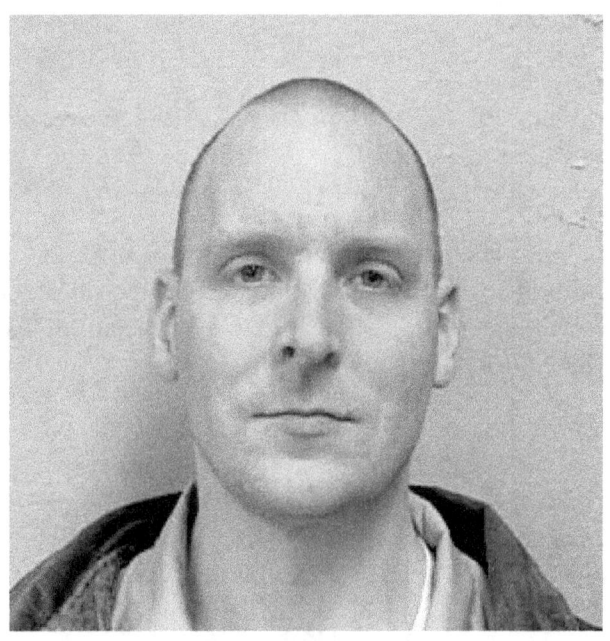

Currently serving a life-without-parole sentence after being wrongfully convicted of a gang-related double murder, Joseph Dole has been continuously incarcerated since 1998. He continues to fight his conviction pro se, as well as fight for both prison reform and criminal justice reform overall.

Joseph Dole spent nearly a decade of his life in the notorious Tamms Supermax Prison, which was shuttered in 2012 after an intense campaign by human rights groups, and the friends and families of the people confined and tortured there.

He has written a number of articles, essays, poems, research papers, and legislative proposals, three of which were catalysts for Illinois legislation (two bills and a resolution). Winner of four different PEN America Writing Awards For Prisoners, his writings have appeared in *The Mississippi Review* (Journal); *The Journal Of Prisoners On Prisons; Scapegoat 7: Incarceration* (Journal); *Lockdown Prison Heart* (Book); *Too Cruel, Not Unusual Enough* (Book); *Hell Is A Very Small Place: Voices From Solitary Confinement* (Book);

Understanding Mass Incarceration: A People's Guide To The Key Civil Rights Struggle Of Our Time (Book); *Prison Legal News* (Magazine); *The Insider* (Magazine); *Stateville Speaks* (Newsletter); *Graterfriends* (Newsletter); *The Public I* (Newspaper); as well as a number of places on-line such as http://www.prisonwriters.com, http://www.realcostofprisons.org, http://www.PrisonLawBlog.com, http://www.*SolitaryWatch.com*, & http://www.allthethingscrimeblog.com.

Currently a writer for *PrisonWriters.com*, Mr. Dole is also author of the self-published *A Costly American Hatred* available at *https://createspace.com/5008773* (ISBN-13: 978-0692298367).

He is both a jailhouse lawyer and jailhouse journalist, as well as a watchdog fighting to ensure that Illinois' government agencies are in compliance with the Illinois Freedom Of Information Act; and is a member of the National Lawyer's Guild.

You can view more of his writings and artwork on Facebook by searching "Joseph Dole Incarcerated Writer" (http://www.facebook.com/JosephDoleIncarceratedWriter); and can contact him via snail mail at the following address and he will respond to all letters he receives.

Joseph Dole K84446
Stateville Correctional Center
P.O.Box 112
Joliet, IL 60434

-ABOUT THE COVER ART & ARTIST-

The artwork used for the cover of this book was designed and painted by artist Matthew Davis. It was done in acrylic paint on a 9" x 12" canvas panel. You can view more of his artwork at *www.hopeforinmates.com*.

Also check out the amazing oil paintings of another (ex-Tamms) prisoner by going to *www.prisoninmates.com/MiguelMorales*.